J. HILLIER

HOKUSAI DRAWINGS

HOKUSAI DRAWINGS

by J. HILLIER

PHAIDON

MADE IN GREAT BRITAIN

PRINTED AND BOUND BY JARROLD AND SONS LTD NORWICH

Foreword

WHATEVER the difference between East and West in concept, media and style—and there are such differences, of course—the Oriental approach to drawing was identical with our own: to translate perception and imagination into pictorial terms. In Japan, as in China, the universal medium was the brush, either with ink, or with colour-washes that approximate to our water-colours, and great stress was placed on *premier coup*, on the brush line itself and on the play of the ink tones. The considered and to us often mannered style of their finished paintings may act as a barrier to our immediate appreciation, but the unpremeditated sketch, the note from nature or the rapid recording of an image of the mind, speaks directly to us in terms we are familiar with. Although it might tax the powers of the most well-meaning internationalist to find common ground between, say, the vast allegorical canvases of Rubens with their crowds of fleshy nudes and the *kakemono* of any Japanese painter of the native schools, it is quite possible to hang a Goya sepia drawing beside a Hokusai sketch in a comparable medium, *sumi*, and to find them perfectly compatible.

In seeking a Japanese parallel to the brush-drawing of a Western master it is perhaps too automatic to think of Hokusai. This is, partly, a hang-over from the wild and indiscriminate praise of this artist's work when the art of Japan first began to attract the notice of Europeans and Americans in the latter half of the last century; and, partly, because in consequence we have become more familiar with his work than with that of equally great Japanese painters (and in the view of some Japanese art-lovers, there are many greater). But it does also reflect, I think, the abiding value of his finest works, and among these the drawings have grown steadily in esteem.

It can be taken for granted that many of those familiar with Japanese painting and the colour-print are aware of the exciting and moving qualities of Hokusai's brush-drawings. The aim of this book is primarily to bring them to the notice of a wider circle, to the lovers of fine drawing generally, whatever the country of origin. Reproduced here on a generous scale, these drawings must make their mark by their expressive line, their vitality, variety of mood and subject, by their revelation of Hokusai the man as well as artist: yet it should be remembered that this is still only a very small fraction of the vast body of Hokusai drawings from which selection has been made.

Any consideration of this artist's drawings is bound up, to a degree inconceivable in relation to any major European artist's work, with the problem of separating them from the mass of copies, forgeries and pupils' paintings which have so often been accepted as Hokusai's in the past. A secondary aim, therefore, has been to reproduce and discuss the drawings of a number of gifted pupils, an acquaintance with whose work will be a novel experience for many, and will help to throw into greater prominence the essential characteristics of Hokusai's own style so providing at least some help towards distinguishing master from pupil, mastery from competence and true from false.

Contents

1. Hokusai and the First Western Contact with Japanese Art

To understand the near-idolatry of Hokusai by the West in the late nineteenth century, and the uncritical acceptance of a great mass of questionable material that ensued, it is worth while considering the peculiar circumstances of the introduction of Japanese art to Europe. Owing to the isolationist policy of the Japanese government, which for centuries practically interdicted communication with the rest of the world, the West had little or no acquaintance with the arts of the country until after the American expedition under Commander Perry in 1853. The belatedness of this contact meant that it came at a time when the whole Western concept of painting was changing under the impact of the Impressionists and their followers. European artists, seeking new horizons, found in the colour-prints of one particular school (the 'Floating World' school) an exemplification of their own half-formulated theories of two dimensional design and non-realistic colour. These prints were of comparatively recent production, and available in great numbers: it was inevitable that *they* should have been brought back to Europe and America rather than the treasured hanging-paintings and the six- and eight-fold screens that were the vehicles of the great Japanese painting of the past. Again, by the middle of the nineteenth century, even before Commander Perry's intimidating squadron had appeared off the Japanese shore, the Japanese had acquired some knowledge, however partial and however clandestinely, of Western styles and techniques, and as the work of the 'Floating World' school was, more than any other, strongly tinged with this Western influence, it was natural that the colour-prints should have appealed more directly to Western taste than the esoteric qualities of essentially Japanese brush-drawing.

The 'Floating World' school was so called because its members depicted the passing show, everyday happenings in the capital, the gay life of courtesans, actors, and the riff-raff of the town. Low-life genre of this kind and the style of semi-representational painting adopted by the artists were both anathema to all Japanese connoisseurs of fine art, and it was incredible to them that the Western world should have admired them as it did, and worse, that foreigners should have accepted the paintings and woodcuts of this school as typical or representative of the nation's art.

Of all the colour-print designers, none made a greater impression on the West than Hokusai, so much so that for some time after the first opening up of Japan to the outside world, his name was almost synonymous with Japanese art, and by a monstrous paradox came to stand for the country's art, although considered by the best native judges to be quite unrepresentative of all that they accepted as most admirable in that art. But the legend of Hokusai's supremacy developed rapidly, until a stage was reached when any drawing that purported to be his had the same efficacy for a dilettante that a relic of saintly bone might have for a good Catholic.

With the passage of time and the greater opportunities to see, if only in reproduction, the masterpieces of classical, as distinct from popular, Japanese painting, there have been attempts to dislodge Hokusai from this position of pre-eminence, but he still obstinately holds a place as one of the incontestably great artists, not simply of Japan, but of the world at large—a view to which the less conservative Japanese now subscribe. It is an interesting exercise in aesthetics to attempt to understand the immense impact of his art on the West in the late nineteenth century and also the change in estimation in the light of greater knowledge today. First we shall try briefly to situate Hokusai's work in the context of Japanese art generally and in the social milieu in which it was produced.

Hokusai, born in 1760, came of artisan stock, relatively low in the social scale. He began work at an early age in a bookseller's shop, went on to serve an apprenticeship with a woodblock-cutter (1774–1777), and in 1777 became a recruit to the 'Floating World' school of artists.

This school had slowly evolved during the seventeenth century after the Tokugawa family had imposed its rule and a measure of peace upon the country, formerly torn by civil wars. The peace led to the emergence of a new class of literate commoner unknown hitherto, which, from what it understood of classical literature and painting and of the ritualistic drama of the nobility, created what may be looked on as its own culture—a racy, picaresque literature, a novel style of painting, and a popular theatre. These were arts practised by the people for the people, and, until the Western world encountered them, were considered trivial and vulgar by all serious Japanese connoisseurs. The 'Floating World' school of painters grew in influence from decade to decade and by Hokusai's day catered for a deep range of strata of the public in Edo, the 'Eastern Capital'. Although most members of the school were painters, it was the woodblock print, and especially the colour-print from woodblocks, that was their special medium, a factor that cannot be too strongly emphasised when considering both the disparagement of their work by the Japanese, and the strength of its impact upon artists and amateurs in the West.

Hokusai's first master, Shunsho, was a designer of theatrical prints, and for a few years the young artist made his way by producing actor prints like those of his master, pictures of the actors in their current roles in the immensely popular Kabuki theatre. He also made the illustrations for the small novelettes known, from the colour of their covers, as 'yellow-backs'. In the next decade his work plainly showed the influence of a number of powerful artists of the 'Floating World' school, and it was not until about 1795 that he began to give evidence of an unmistakably personal style. This coincided with new activities in designing prints for special occasions (*surimono*), small pictures with accompanying verses for the purpose of invitation, congratulation, or New Year's Day, good wishes and also prints for albums of light verse then being produced by the bohemian intelligentsia of the capital.

Simultaneously, Hokusai began to study other styles of painting: Chinese, the ancient Japanese, the decorative works of followers of the seventeenth century painters Sotatsu and Korin, even European art through examples imported by Dutch traders. But whatever he may have absorbed from these diverse sources served, if anything, only to accentuate the eccentricities of his own style.

By 1800, Hokusai was established and extremely active as painter, print designer, and illustrator of novels and albums of verse. Slowly, his own especial bent for landscape became apparent. In the first decade of the new century he designed colour-prints for a number of books that had Edo and its environs as their subject, of which 'Panoramic Views Along Both Banks of the Sumida River' is typical. In these early landscapes, human incident was still Hokusai's main preoccupation, and the landscape itself, though it provided a quasi-topographical setting for the figures, relatively unimportant. In the next ten years, a marked change occurred in Hokusai's outdoor pictures, the bias shifting from the figures to the scenic features, until, in the justly famous series of prints, the 'Thirty-six Views of Fuji', there are designs, like the 'Shower below the Summit', for example, in which no human being disturbs the serenity and sublimity of the landscapes.

From the time of the Fuji set until his death in 1849, Hokusai produced the prints on which his fame largely rests. Contrary to popular belief, they are not particularly numerous. Apart from the forty-six prints of the Fuji set, there were sets of eight and ten respectively devoted to Waterfalls and Bridges; eleven 'Large' Flowers and ten 'Small' Flowers (distinguished by the format of the prints); eight 'Views of the Luchu Islands'; twenty-seven of a series illustrating classical poetry entitled, 'The One-hundred Poems explained by the Nurse'; ten of a *kakemono* or 'hanging picture' format, also based on the poetry of China and Japan (the 'Imagery of the Poets'), and half-a-dozen in the same format of varying subject matter; a set of ten with ocean or riverside subjects, with the unexplained title of the 'The Ocean of a Thousand Ideas'; and a hundred or so of other prints of a miscellaneous nature. (This does not take into account the very considerable number of *surimono* designed by Hokusai at all periods throughout his career.)

Actually, Hokusai's greatest activity, even allowing for his considerable output of screens and *kakemono*, was in the field of book-illustration. Apart from the albums of verse already mentioned, there were immensely long novels and, more important, 'picture-books' (*ehon*), compilations of a type unique to Japan and consisting of series of often quite disconnected sketches reproduced by woodblock. Few people ever have the time or opportunity to get to know more than a part of the books with illustrations by Hokusai (well over two hundred in number, many composed of several volumes), but one above all was acclaimed by the West—the 'Miscellaneous Sketches' (*Manga*), issued at intervals from 1814 and reaching a total of thirteen volumes during the artist's lifetime. The *Manga* is an enormous encyclopaedia of everything under the Japanese sun, and everything in Japanese legend, history and ghost-lore besides. It is an incredible, ill-organised jumble, full of an old man's whimsicalities, but above all demonstrating his wonderful fertility of invention and amazing ability to impart life and movement to figures.

It is this same quality of life and movement that made Hokusai's brush-drawings immediately acceptable to the Western world: they spoke a language little removed from that of certain European artists. This compatability is to a certain extent an accident of the similarity of the medium used by Hokusai and Rembrandt or Goya or many other Western artists. Hokusai's brush style was truly Oriental in the sense that spirit was always more essential than mere imitation. He remained to the end of his days an indifferent draughtsman by any standard based solely on literal representation—he often drew hands badly and his unclothed figures, if closely examined, reveal a bone structure and an anatomy generally that is far from that of *homo sapiens*. But despite what, in a Western artist of his period, we would sense as failings, Hokusai still overwhelms us, in his finest brush-drawings, with a dynamism, a vitality, the creation of a sense of life as well as a feeling for the brush-line itself, that reduce the criticism of details to pedantry.

It is perhaps to be expected that, in view of the *éclat* of his prints, his drawings should also have been feverishly sought after: though curiously enough, the drawings, for all their verve and their innate sense of composition, lack the very attributes of the colour-print which were causing the excitement and which were largely the outcome of the colour-print medium and the cutters and printers who exercised the craft so superbly. The drawings have, in fact, made their way into Western affection by virtue of qualities that evoke chords from the same strings in our beings that respond to the drawings of great Western draughtsmen; the *Manga* simply reproduced in woodcut the brush-drawings. The colour-woodcuts, on the other hand, in broadsheet or in such books as the 'One-hundred Views of Fuji', represented something entirely unprecedented, and certainly accelerated the pace at which Western artists at the end of the nineteenth century moved away from 'representation for its own sake' towards a concept in which the artists, not nature, dictated what form a picture should take.

Perhaps Hokusai's impact has lost its impetus now, and what he could teach us has become part of the repertoire of every student artist. The novelty of Hokusai, and of the Japanese print generally, begins to wear off. But though this may be admitted, there is no call to think the less of the splendid legacy of this artist and his fellows: the novelty of Cézanne, too, has worn off, his influence on the trend of art is a matter of history, but his paintings can still be enjoyed even if they are no longer the rallying point for revolutionaries. We are able now to accept Hokusai's prints and drawings not for their influence on the course of Western painting and design, but simply as works of art in their own right, and an anthology of his drawings, such as I have attempted to make here, surely proves that it would be difficult to deny him a place among the great artists of the world.

2. Hokusai's Drawings: Some Problems of Attribution

As I have hinted, it is with something like arrogance that we in the West admit Hokusai into the select company of the world's greatest artists. He spoke a brush language we understand. In rather the same patronising way, we evaluate the music of countries of the East: where the mode, the musical interval, and the instruments are sufficiently akin to our own, the pleasure of recognising a likeness to something we know leads us to praise, but other music that has little relation to our own we ignore as incomprehensible, or despise as barbaric.

The art of the painters most esteemed in the East, both in China and Japan, is a conscious and studied employment of brush-stroke and ink-tones, often leading to results which to the European or American, ignorant of the Oriental aim and tradition of style, seem bizarre, eccentric or daringly impressionistic. In some of his screens and *kakemono*, those paintings in fact that may be considered the most seriously conceived products of his art, it is evident that Hokusai was vying with the masters traditionally revered in Japan, and these paintings fail to please either the purists in his own country, who are immediately aware of the shortcomings of his brushwork, or the Western admirers of his prints and drawings, who sense, though they cannot perhaps explain, something foreign and apart in such screens and *kakemono* which is absent, or less pronounced, in the colour-prints and the unpremeditated drawings.

But from the very first acquaintance of the West with the world of Japanese art, Hokusai's brush-drawings, as distinct from the paintings proper, have been admired and sought after. What is their appeal to us, and how much of it is due to the fact that, unlike much Oriental painting, their idiom needs no interpreting, no mental focusing to bring it into our normal range? Hokusai had not imbibed more of European tendencies than his contemporaries, though he had, like a number of others, superficially studied Occidental methods. Our admiration seems to have been aroused because he used the brush to record people and things around him with a naturalism, a spontaneity, and a convention of line far nearer to our own kind of drawing than to the mannered Oriental styles, in which representation may be considered secondary to brushwork, just as, in a page of their handwriting, meaning may be sacrificed to calligraphic bravura.

In his drawings, especially those free sketches which were either made directly from the model or with it freshly in mind, Hokusai used his brush as unconsciously as Rembrandt or Goya. Varied brush-line and subtleties of ink-tone were not his first aim, but instead his intent was to record, to capture on the wing, the visual appearance of anything and everything that passed before his inquisitive eyes, to give visible existence to characters, and scenes of history and legend with which his whimsical imagination teemed. His method was largely linear, or line and wash, and chiaroscuro as a scientific matter of light and shade was ignored, his effects being obtained by the thickening or thinning of the line or by the arbitrary placing of dark or light patches of ink: but this is the method, *mutatis mutandis*, of all those we admire most in the West as draughtsmen with the brush, Rembrandt for example, or Claude, Goya, Guardi or Cozens. To say he used the brush 'unconsciously' is not to imply he was without real feeling for the medium, but simply that it was to him, as to the Western artists named, a means to an end: an incident in the road, an event in a novel, a landscape, called for the drawing; they were not motives for the display of brushwork. The instrument was played for the music, not to exhibit the executant's virtuosity. Paradoxically, what matters to us is not the subject primarily, but the qualities that, without the artist's being conscious of them, develop as soon as he puts brush-tip to paper.

But although Hokusai has earned a place, in our estimation at least, as one of the greatest of brush draughtsmen, it is a strange fact that more controversy is aroused concerning the authenticity of drawings attributed to him than has arisen in respect of the drawings of any other artist of the same stature. When we mention the drawings of Leonardo, or Rembrandt, or Dürer, a body of drawings is in our minds, universally accepted and forming the very basis upon which their assessment as great draughtsmen rests. But mention the drawings of Hokusai, and it is unlikely that any two Orientalists will agree upon those that might be accepted as the canon to justify the claim to rank the Japanese master so highly.

Several factors, apart from the enormous bulk of so-called Hokusai drawings, have operated to cause this lack of unanimity. At the end of the nineteenth century, when the West suddenly became aware of the pictorial greatness of Japan, the infatuation of the various amateurs and artists—mostly in France—who first came under the spell, was rarely accompanied by what we would now call a critical apparatus. So far as the colour-prints were concerned, few problems of attribution arose, as they were almost invariably signed, but the drawings and sketches rarely bore the signature of the artist; or where they did, such signatures could not be relied on, and, at a time when everything was new and delightful, there existed neither the knowledge, nor the means of acquiring the knowledge, by which one artist's work could be distinguished from another's, at any rate where the two were contemporary and brought up in the same school. Prominent first as a print-designer, work of Hokusai's in the brush medium was soon eagerly sought, and the collections of such pioneers as Gonse, Bing, and de Goncourt were swollen by large numbers of drawings assigned to him, some with good reason, others on what we now feel to be insufficient grounds. The weight of these early ascriptions has been instrumental in holding together under Hokusai's name a multitude of drawings, so varied in style and content that, however phenomenal an artist he may have been, it is impossible to accept them all as his handiwork. The interest of dealers in maintaining the *status quo* has also to be taken into account, and as the expertise has been lacking to determine any universally acceptable guide to authenticity, more and more drawings have been added through the years to the original nucleus, so that now a vast number pass for Hokusai's, of which probably only a small proportion were actually from his hand.

Another factor that has to be taken into account is the Japanese system of tutelage for artists. Where much stress was laid on a *style* of brushwork, it was the pupil's aim to be able to make a drawing that would be indistinguishable from the master's. Individuality, the very basis of our differentiation between one artist and another, was not merely unlikely in a pupil, it was deliberately suppressed. To go no further back than the eighteenth century, or no further afield than the colour-prints, everyone knows how notoriously difficult it is to distinguish between unsigned prints of Harunobu and his pupils, or of Shunsho and his. Even when an artist had reached his maturity and had passed the need for instruction, it was not considered beneath him to copy an admired master's painting or drawing. From the earliest times, such copying had been encouraged as a mark of respect or homage, and the accuracy of the replica was a measure of the compliment:

indeed, it would be hard to say how many great artists' works are known, not through originals, though they are often accepted as such, but through copies by gifted followers of originals that have been lost.

At a time when the Ukiyo-e school was in a decline, Hokusai not only added lustre to its name by his own achievements, but attracted into his orbit many of the finest talents of his day and gave instruction to men who maintained a certain integrity in their work during a period of generally falling standards. An immensely long list of artists can be compiled who may be said to have enrolled themselves under his leadership, though in what way, and to what extent, his instruction was given we have little knowledge. Here it is only necessary to mention Soji, the artist to whom Hokusai gave his early name of Sori; Hokkei; Hokuba; Taito (Hokusen); Hokuga; Yanagawa Shigenobu; Oei, his daughter; and Isai—a group which, judging by their engraved works and in some cases by their paintings, came nearest to acquiring and repeating Hokusai's style and mannerisms. I shall deal more fully with some of these artists later, but here I will simply draw attention to the paucity of extant brush-drawings considered to be by them. The public collections of the world can only muster a handful and these are always signed: the unavoidable inference being that unsigned drawings by these artists have invariably been fathered upon Hokusai. The engraved work of several of these artists forms a considerable bulk, most of them were active for long periods, and though none of them achieved anything like the fame of Hokusai, it is difficult to accept the view that their output in the brush medium was so small, or, if greater, that so little should have been preserved.

Apprentice pupils in Hokusai's studio were set to copy his drawings. Some drawings, we know, were made specially for this purpose. Three or four sketches were angled about a single sheet of paper in such a way that several pupils could work from the same exemplar at the same time. Copying these drawings time after time, it is quite likely that a talented pupil would repeat the original with a fair show of plausibility, and this replica would obviously be the one that the pupil would be most likely to retain. In other countries, the practice of artists' providing drawing-copies for their pupils has also led to confusion between master's and pupil's work. To take only one example, it is now thought that large numbers of the sepia drawings ascribed to Cotman are probably by the aptest of those amateurs to whom he gave drawing lessons.

Nor is it only the pupils and followers of Hokusai whose work is liable to be mistaken for the master's. Other contemporary artists of the Ukiyo-e school were capable of fine brush-drawing, and in particular, Kuniyoshi, of the Utagawa sub-school, might be cited as one who, by a certain vitality and fluency in brushwork, a spontaneity that, like Hokusai's, breaks down the barrier between East and West and makes his drawings as readily accessible to us as those of his older contemporary, produced drawings that can be confused with Hokusai's.

The last factor to be mentioned as contributing to the confusion is what might be called the 'traffic' in Hokusai drawings. The wish to possess autographed works of the great master having always been so widespread, it is not surprising that unscrupulous methods were introduced to satisfy the demand. Old sketch-books, known, perhaps, to be by other artists, were broken up, and the loose sheets passed off as Hokusai's; drawings by unknown hands were given spurious signatures; and worse, new drawings made by skilful imitators, sometimes with sufficient of Hokusai's manner to tempt the unwary, appeared as 'preparatory studies' for *Manga* and other woodcuts (woodcuts made, of course, many years before the drawings). These forgeries and deceptions, of a kind not peculiar to Japanese art, serve to make still more complicated a matter already beset by problems enough, so much so that a discussion of Hokusai's drawings becomes almost a case of '*il ne faut pas vendre la peau de l'ours avant qu'il n'ait été tué*'.

From the foregoing it will be clear that no reliance can be placed on signatures or seals as a means of authentication, though both are of great value, when the drawing is accepted, in placing it roughly in a chronological sequence. Signatures and seals could be, and were, added not merely to drawings plainly not from Hokusai's hand but to perfectly genuine, unsigned, works—and the dealers, making doubly sure, as they thought, more often than not cast doubts upon a good drawing by appending signature and seals which did not 'match'. Some critics, it is true, have approached the whole problem of authentication largely on the basis of signatures and the correspondence of the seals which should correctly be found with particular signatures, but the fact that any signature is easier to imitate than a drawing, and that seals could be manufactured to order and the originals themselves sometimes continued to exist after an artist's death, had led me, in my inquiry, to ignore them as far as possible and to attempt to find the unique touch, the sign manual, in the drawings themselves.

How, then, it may justly be asked—and is asked continually by collectors—how are we ever to be sure that any drawing is in truth from Hokusai's hand? We cannot point to this or that feature and say 'only Hokusai could have drawn that'. Many of the drawings are instinct with drollery, whimsicality, and a wide sympathy for humanity, especially the lower orders, but though Hokusai had these characteristics superabundantly, he had no monopoly of them, for they inform the work of most Japanese artists, not merely of the Ukiyo-e school; again, the heads and limbs of the human beings are drawn in a fashion that seems to segregate the owners, anatomically, from the rest of mankind, but these men and women, although Hokusai's creation originally, were reproduced with an uncanny family likeness in the woodcuts and drawings of Hokkei, Taito II, and other pupils, and the presence of *homo Hokusaiensis* in a drawing by no means confirms Hokusai as the artist.

In the end, I think one is forced in many instances to rely on an inner conviction of authenticity, a recognition of some quality which, like the timbre of a voice, is utterly personal without being definable. This may seem like an uncritical surrender to a kind of sixth sense, but it is one that only develops after seeing a great many so-called Hokusai drawings, and until some more scientific means can be devised, it seems that we shall have to rely on what, at best, can only be an inspired empiricism.

3. Hokusai's Drawings: The Early Period

DATING of Hokusai's drawings up to the year 1839 (after which he made a practice of always signing his full pictures, and sometimes his drawings) is normally on internal evidence: comparison with the rare dated painting or, more frequently, with prints in illustrated books, which were usually dated and of which there are a great number covering all periods of the artist's life. The first attempts to impose some sort of chronology on the mass of extant works were made by Fenollosa on the occasion of two comprehensive exhibitions of Hokusai's paintings, the first at Boston in 1893, the second, and far more valuable, in Tokyo in 1900. His catalogues for these exhibitions are the foundation of every subsequent study of the artist's work. We may today differ from him with regard to a few of his ascriptions and dates, but by and large his wide experience and opportunity to compare and select from great numbers of drawings, ensured that the exhibits passed a stiff test of authenticity. Some of the drawings in the 1900 exhibition, then in the possession of Kobayashi, had been obtained many years earlier from the house of a well-known pupil of Hokusai, Isai, with whom Hokusai had actually lived for some time. If we are to consider provenance at all—and often where there is a shade of indecision or doubt, it may give as it were a casting vote—then the 1900 exhibition carries considerable weight, and fortunately, several of the exhibits passed to Mr. Freer, and can be seen today in the Freer Gallery in Washington. Many of my reproductions are, therefore, from this more or less unimpeachable source.

Kyosai, the popular painter of the late nineteenth century, was that unusual exception among Japanese artists, a collector of Ukiyo-e paintings and prints, and he treasured among his possession a large number of Hokusai paintings and drawings which, it seems likely, must have come to him at first remove from Hokusai himself. Certain of these too came to Europe through such collectors as Gonse, and in particular, a wonderful water-colour scroll of flowers, birds, and insects, which will be mentioned later.

The drawings divide themselves into several groups. There are random sketches, thrown off without apparently any premeditated plan for use; preparatory drawings for book-illustrations and colour-prints, either first draughts or re-drawn with the needs of the block-cutter in mind; others that might be termed 'presentation' drawings, carried out with a more than usual degree of care and finish, intended to stand on their own feet as drawings and so lying mid-way between the rough sketch and the elaborated *kakemono* painting. There are, too, wash drawings in monochrome and colour that stand rather outside the general classifications, and paintings which, although mounted as *kakemono*, retain the especial and characteristic verve of the artist's most uninhibited style of drawing.

It is not possible to deal with these groups with anything like strict chronological progression because, for one reason and another, few drawings have survived from the earliest period in the artist's career when he was first apprentice and then minor practitioner in the Ukiyo-e school, and successively under the influence of Shunsho, Kiyonaga and Utamaro, the predominant masters of the school during his formative years. Drawings of the time with which we are concerned—say, 1790 to 1800—had little or no value outside Hokusai's immediate circle and even had he been of far greater stature than he was, there was no tradition of collecting drawings of an ephemeral character that would have ensured the preservation of a body of them. Moreover, there is record of a fire in 1839 which consumed all the old artist's possessions, including no doubt a lifetime's hoard of drawings. The great majority of extant drawings belong to the last decade of the artist's life, after the date—in fact, again 1839—when he began to make a regular practice of signing and dating at least his finished works.

In view of the paucity of chance sketches of the earliest period, I am illustrating the years just before and after 1800 by a few *kakemono* and a fan. Generally, these *kakemono* —to a certain extent 'commissioned' paintings—will seem restrained in handling compared with the casual sketches that have survived of later years.

The first (plate 1), a *kakemono* in the Hakone Museum, is unsigned, but the features of the girl reflected in the mirror, and the long body and short legs, remind us at once of the *musume* types in book and print, especially *surimono*, appearing at the turn of the century under the signatures of Sori or Gakyojin Hokusai. It is freer in handling than was customary in the stock Ukiyo-e painting of the period, and has to that extent greater affinity with later drawings than certain more orthodox paintings such as the 'Two Beauties' also in Hakone or the 'Courtesan and Attendants' in Boston. There is a suspicion of moistness in the washes, and the lines of the *kimono*, at the neck for instance, have that fluid, calligraphic undulation which is the basis of much of our pleasure in Hokusai's drawings.

The drawing of the foppish young man (plate 2) is even freer, and shows already, at this comparatively early date (about 1797), how expressive Hokusai could be with a few suggestive brush lines and massive washes, which seem to have been slashed on with impatient gusto, but which, looked at more closely, are seen to suggest the bend of the arm, the fall of the silk. Fenollosa put his finger on one of the felicities of this and other drawings of the period when he wrote 'colour seems to grow gradually out of the paper'. The colour is subtle and unobtrusive, and the next *bijin-ga* ('beautiful-girl picture') exemplifies this to perfection. This *kakemono* (plate 5) is a splendid creation, and the figure is so fully worked out that it perhaps passes beyond the limits we have in mind when we use the word drawing: but those limits are anything but hard and fast, and the line plays so prominent a part in this painting that it is difficult to deny it a place.

It is interesting to note that all three of these drawings have (or had) inscriptions by Santo Kyoden, who, apart from his ability as an artist himself, was one of the most gifted literary figures of the Edo of this time, and a man with whom Hokusai clearly had the strongest ties. (Although the Freer painting of the young fop does not show an inscription, it has presumably been hidden by the mount or trimmed off, since it is visible in the reproduction in the 1900 catalogue, to the right of the figure.)

I am inclined to place the 'Woman dressing her hair' (plate 7) at or soon after the time of these *bijin-ga*. The drawing of the nude body has none of the curious articulation that developed later in Hokusai's rendering of the figure, and indeed it is not characteristically his at all; on the other hand, the accurately observed pose and the effective sweep of line in the clothes covering the girl's lower limbs are within the competence of no other Ukiyo-e painter at this period, and somehow it does not strike me as other than Ukiyo-e. Hair-styles are of inestimable value in helping to date Japanese drawings, but here the coiffure, half-finished and seen from behind, does not give any conclusive indication.

The two drawings of flowering plum (plates 6, 8) are also of about 1798. It was a time when Hokusai, aside from his Ukiyo-e work, was practising a style of painting under the name Sori that harked back to Sotatsu and his successors, his immediate mentor being an obscure artist who had earlier employed the same name Sori. This school, only inter-mittently active in a broken line from the time of Sotatsu in the seventeenth century, gave to Japanese painting its especially decorative bias, evolving, from a fusion of Chinese and early native painting, in conjunction with a study of nature, a power of matchless composition and patterned colour that we recognise now as one of the unique gifts of Japanese art to the world. Hokusai's debt to this school comes out particularly in certain of his *surimono*, especially those in the long, narrow format used, among other things, as a means of publishing *kyoka*, the 'crazy' verse produced by the *literati* of the 'Floating World'; and is likewise apparent in prints that embellished albums of *kyoka* contributed by the same dilettante versifiers.

The hanging painting (plate 6) was one of the glories of the collection formed by Louis Gonse, one of the first to appreciate the essentially Japanese qualities of the Korin style. It has a refinement, a serene decorativeness, that quite belie the notion that those brought up in the Ukiyo-e tradition were incapable of the deep feeling, the spirit as well as the evocative line or wash, that belonged to the classic masters and the artists of poetic decora-tion. The fan (plate 8), though no more than a trifle, is a minor masterpiece of the period.

There is small doubt that in this formative period, Hokusai was trying his hand at a variety of styles, and the landscape (plate 9), one of the earliest pure landscapes surviving, is evidence of experiment in a style of painting called *haboku*, 'splash ink', the greatest exponents of which were to be found in the classical Kano school, whose inspiration, at bottom, came from China. This is a charming wash-drawing, but, like one or two attempts by Utamaro to vie with the great masters of ink-painting, has probably been over-praised. 'The free velvety touch with which deep crisp inks are thrown into crumbling greys' results in a lovely atmospheric drawing, but it hardly reminds me, as it did Fenollosa, of Sesshu.

Three other drawings (plates 10–12) of about this period or a little later, say 1805–1812, are reproduced. In these, the style and brushwork are far from the orthodox Ukiyo-e, the paintings relying on broad transparent washes more in common with the method of the Shijo school of artists than the decided outline and opaque colour typical of Ukiyo-e painting proper. The dating of these drawings, it is true, is dependent to a certain extent on the signatures and seals, but on other counts they fit into this period of experimentation when Hokusai showed his independence of any strict allegiance to one school by running the gamut of current painting styles. This in itself marks Hokusai off from the great majority of Japanese artists of the time, who rarely went beyond the confines of the accepted style of their school, and it is yet another obstacle to any approach to Hokusai's drawings on the grounds of style alone.

The Metropolitan Museum's fine preparatory drawing (plate 15) for an illustration to Rokujuen's novel *Hida-no-Takumi Monogatari,* 'The Story of the Hida Craftsman', published in 1808, brings me to the question of drawings made for the block-cutters, whether for book illustration or single sheets. For long it was assumed that in the production of a woodcut the artist's drawing was pasted on to the block and destroyed in the process of cutting, but far too many drawings of which engraved versions are known have come to light for this practice to have been universal. From Kiyonaga's time at least it seems to have been the artists' practice to prepare a first draft that gave the broad outline of the woodcut, omitting repetitive detail like patterns on clothes, foliage of trees, or the tiles of a roof. Of the first drawing, either the artist, or someone in the block-cutter's workshop, would make a careful copy, filling in the detail, and this drawing would be pasted on to the block and destroyed in the woodcutting. It is perhaps surprising how few of the original first drafts have survived, but there is ample evidence that, before Hokusai's time certainly, they were considered of little account, and of those that exist, many have owed their preservation to chance. A fine drawing by Kiyonaga, for instance, now in the British Museum, a preparatory sketch for the print of 'Murasame and Matsukaze', was rescued from the binding of an album.

The *Hida-no-Takumi* drawing (plate 15), made carefully for the block-cutter, may not bring out Hokusai's growing freedom with the brush at the time (1808), but it does give evidence of a gift for composition, for the creation of monumental design from the elements provided by novelists like Rokujuen and Bakin, of whom (despite Bakin's protestations to the contrary) Hokusai was so splendid an illustrator.

Two further drawings in the Metropolitan Museum (plates 14, 16) are clearly allied to the last and are probably also drawings for book-illustrations, though I have not come across them in any of the illustrated novels known to me. Somewhat akin are the drawings in an album of uncommon interest in the Harari collection (plates 17–20). There are eight drawings in the album, on very thin paper, such as was used where the drawings were to be pasted on to the block. *Sumi* is used throughout, with the addition of colour in one instance only (plate 18). In that drawing the colour is limited to a blue wash for the water. The drawings are unsigned, but there can be little doubt as to the artist. Fortunately, one of the drawings is dated, almost accidentally it would seem. In the 'Ferry Boat' (plate 18) there is a square inset bearing the sign *Uru* (intercalary) followed by the figure 2. In the Japanese calendar of that period, an Intercalary Month was added in certain years with the same object as our extra day in Leap Years. The Japanese Intercalary was named with reference to the month it followed, and hence Intercalary 2 meant between Second and Third. On the drawing in question, it could only refer to the year 1811 which was the only year during Hokusai's lifetime when an Intercalary fell between the Second and Third months. However curiously inserted, there seems no reason to doubt the validity of the dating, which is in fact confirmed by the style of the drawing, a logical development from the Metropolitan's *Hida-no-Takumi* sketch.

The drawings belong, therefore, to an interesting transitional phase of Hokusai's style concerning which we know very little: a phase falling in the period that saw the last of the great illustrated novels and the first *Manga* volume of 1814. Hardly any drawings have survived from this period. Even the 1900 Tokyo exhibition had no drawing certainly attributable to the year 1811, and Fenollosa was able to ascribe only six of the drawings exhibited to the period 1810 to 1812.

The equality in size and the obvious linkage between the subjects suggest that the drawings were the first draughts, *shita-e*, for a series of colour-prints devoted to 'Occupations of the "Floating World"' or something of that nature. No prints based on these drawings are known. There is no doubt that many sets of prints were projected that never got beyond the roughing-out stage. Fenollosa, in his preface to the 1900 catalogue, wrote: 'Hokusai was so prolific a designer that he often executed masses of sketches more or less rough, throwing them aside in heaps until he should want them or the right occasion for publishing should occur. We know this from the number of such studies in series that even now turn up, series which have never been printed.'

The 'Occupations' are full of lively incident and movement and the figures come well to the fore. They predominate over the landscape more than they do in the topographical picture books of a few years earlier, or even the Chushingura set of 1806. However, a simplification of the landscape, and a concentration on the drama in that setting, point to the development that was to lead to the superb *Gashiki* of 1819, a picture-book in which the figures completely fill the pages in a most commanding way. Plate 47, from a preparatory study for one of the *Gashiki* designs, shows the connection with the 'Occupations', and the immense assurance which succeeded the slightly tentative handling of the earlier drawings.

Nonetheless, the reproductions from the 'Occupations' album (plates 17–20) show how fluent Hokusai's brush had become by 1811, how easily he described chance movements —the casualness of the seated porter at the quayside (plate 17) for example, or the strain of the ferryman pushing off from the bank (plate 18). Historically, these drawings are clearly interesting to the student, but that is of secondary importance: by reason of the quality of their line they are immediately acceptable to all who care for fine drawing.

Quite a number of extant Hokusai drawings are either first sketches made with print or book-illustration in mind (plate 13), or carefully worked out drawings in which firm lines suitable for the guidance of the block-cutter have been brought out of the nebulous maze of strokes in the original sketch, often, of course, with great loss of spirit and sacrifice of the master's touch.

Drawings exist for the great colour-print series entitled 'The Thirty-six Views of Fuji', but though one might have expected them to be among the most memorable of Hokusai's drawings, none of them is anything like as impressive as the woodcut for which it was the first draught. Bearing in mind what has been said above, this is not surprising. The woodcut was conceived in the artist's mind as something depending for its effect as much on the pattern of the block-printed colours as on the outline, and the actual brush strokes were no more than an outline guide, the drawings being simply 'working drawings' for the block-cutter. Nor can we always be sure that the final version of the drawing for the cutter was Hokusai's own. The fact that cutters' drawings exist at all seems to prove that more than one copy was made at times, and such copies may have been made in the publisher's studio. This copy-work would have been the ideal apprenticeship for a would-be artist, such an apprenticeship, or something akin, was, in fact, Hokusai's own introduction to Ukiyo-e. Drawings copied in this way lack the original verve, the very soul of the brush-line, as difficult to reproduce as another person's handwriting.

The two drawings known as 'The Mad Poet' instance the kind of enfeeblement that occurs when a free-drawn sketch is copied, even well-copied. The one, once in the collection of Mrs. Seligman and then of Madame Berès (plate 21), seems spontaneous, with a dashing line thrown on to the paper at the pace of the artist's inspiration. The other, in the British Museum (plate 22) fine as it is, seems an obvious copy by a brush that is cool and collected and able to correct the faults that impetuosity gave rise to in the first attempt. The result is a suave, accomplished piece of work that, to my mind, pales before the other.

An even clearer example is provided by a comparison of the drawings in the British Museum for the *Ehon Suikoden* (plates 38–39) and the unfinished *makimono* in the Freer Gallery (plate 40) which is obviously based on these drawings. Whether or not the Freer *makimono* is actually from the hand of Hokusai (and neither the completed portion nor the brush-outlined remainder convinces me), one can at least see the effect of a patient transcription from an original, the quenching of that vital spark that animates the British Museum drawings. Indeed, more of the original character is retained in the wood-cuts made from the British Museum drawings (which are referred to again in the next chapter).

4. Hokusai's Drawings: 1814–1839

IN 1814, the first of the *Manga* volumes appeared, and as these were simply woodcut transcriptions of 'rough sketches', from this time on we have a fairly good idea of certain facets of Hokusai's style, his personal quirks in regard to subject, and the flavour of his work as a whole. I have already mentioned preparatory drawings for book illustration, to which Hokusai was evidently devoting the greater part of his energies during a period from about 1800 to 1814. It is to the years subsequent to the end of this bout of book-illustration that one of the outstanding albums of Hokusai drawings can be ascribed: that in the John T. Spaulding collection in the Museum of Fine Arts, Boston, known as 'Day and Night in the Four Seasons'. These drawings, ninety-six in number, have the strongest possible claims to authenticity. One of them is signed Hokusai and has the seal Katsushika Hokusai (plate 27); another is sealed Fujiyama, one of the many seals used by Hokusai at different times in his career (plate 30); and accompanying the album is a note from the hand of Tanseido Hokuyo Shigeyoshi, one of Hokusai's pupils, certifying that the album drawings are 'from the brush of Master Katsushika I-itsu'. This note is dated 11th Month of the 3rd year of Tempo (1832), but Hokusai's signatures and seals on the drawings themselves predicate a date much earlier than 1832. Mr. Tomita[1] concludes that they belong to the year 1819, but he bases his finding partly on signatures not on the drawings themselves, but attached to the containing box, and I think on the evidence of the names and seals on the drawings that a date nearer 1815 would be more likely.

Be that as it may, the set is of the utmost interest and importance, and, as can be seen from the reproductions (plates 26–33), marks a distinct departure from all foregoing drawings, and, indeed, amounts to something unique in Hokusai's oeuvre, both in scope and style. Hokusai developed so wide a variety of styles over his long career that it is not impossible to find something in his original or printed works akin to almost any drawing which had sufficient character to justify an ascription to his hand, and Mr. Tomita points to Volumes VIII–X of the *Manga*, published in 1818-1819, as containing pictures not unlike the sketches under discussion. However, even when due allowance has been made for the change brought about by the translation into the woodcut medium, none of the drawings in the *Manga* has quite the loose freedom, the entire absence of mannerism, of the 'Day and Night' drawings. (*Cf.* plates 24–25 from the *Manga* VIII.) There is none of that curiously artificial marking of the limbs that normally stamps a figure as of the Hokusai tribe: a 'Sudden Shower' (plate 26) shows on the contrary an unaccountable amorphousness in the limbs—all that remains to confirm Hokusai as the artist is the infallible rendering of the figures in motion, and the gift of pictorial spacing. Plates 26-33 are all lovely and inimitable drawings—but still hard to square with the notions most people have of Hokusai's style.

One even wonders whether the apartness of this set of drawings may not have been the result of its having been a special commission—the working out so thoroughly of the theme of 'Day and Night', with all the multifarious occupations and amusements and festivals of the common people suggests either a scheme for a picture-book (which certainly never materialised), or an album of connected drawings on the theme of the 'Floating World in Edo', proposed by a patron who may also in some way have inspired the unusual idiom of the drawings. Whatever the genesis, it is one of the most wonderful collections of Hokusai drawings extant, and the touches of colour in a low key—Venetian red and two shades of grey-blue—give some of them a beauty rare among the countless works of the artist. It is, too, an epitome of this eccentric old man's view of his fellow-men. He was about fifty-four or fifty-five when it was compiled, he had been an Edo man all his life, and he intended the album to be a compendium of all the activities, day and night, of the people he knew best, the working people of the town, the tradesmen, the craftsmen, the merchants, the mendicant monks, the courtesans, the pimps. But there was that streak of the humorist in Hokusai that is forever coming out in the events and incidents he singles out to draw. The bent coolie, struggling along with *sake* at each end of the yoke across his neck, stops to

[1] 'Day and Night in the Four Seasons: Sketches by Hokusai 1760–1849', Museum of Fine Arts, Boston, 1957.

watch two carefree little girls kneeling to bounce a ball; in a yard where umbrella-makers are drying their wares, great play (pictorially as well as anecdotally) is made of the umbrella that is caught up in a gust of wind and knocks a man sideways (plate 32); in another, a woman at one side is buying tiny mushrooms held out in a tray for her inspection whilst, on the other, four men are straining their hearts out to move a great boulder of rock on a trolley; the trifling and the portentous are forever mingling as they must have done in the crowded streets of Edo, and Hokusai's observant commentary catches something of the true comic spirit that plays over the crowd scenes of all great artists, in literature or painting.

Some of the problems of the period under review arise over the use of the name Taito by Hokusai from 1811 until 1819, and the taking over of this name from 1819 onwards by a gifted but unscrupulous pupil, Hokusen. Unscrupulous, not because he assimilated more closely than other pupils the style and idiosyncrasies of composition of his master, but because he deliberately forged signatures to which he had been given no patent, with the object of passing off his own prints as if they were Hokusai's. More will be said of Taito II in Chapter 6, but his proved frauds cast more than a doubt not so much on drawings that bear the signature Taito as on those that came later when Hokusai had adopted the name I-itsu.

But there is none the less the difficulty of distinguishing between the paintings and drawings of the two artists when they bear the signature Taito. Plate 36 is from a painting that is unmistakably from Hokusai's brush: the technique of this highly finished *kakemono* does not admit the doubt which may legitimately arise in relation to many an unpremeditated drawing. This *kakemono* is signed Zen (formerly) Hokusai Taito, and it is sealed with the same seal that we saw used in the 'Day and Night' drawing (plate 30). It is instructive, and possibly a little chastening, to compare this painting with another (plate 37) of only a few years later, so much fresher and more ardent than the earlier that it is hard to be forced to accept it as the work of the miscreant pupil: yet such I am sure it is. The signature is Taito, but it is written in what must be—even to those unfamiliar with Japanese calligraphy—obviously a different hand from that which signed the other painting; and the seal is Taito, which I have not found recorded among the seals used by Hokusai. Hokusai's 'Courtesan Making a New Year Visit' was clearly a 'set piece', and it lacks just those qualities which, in the drawings, we find immediately attractive. It is refreshing to look again at that lively drawing of bakers at work (plate 47) drawn more or less at the same time as the Courtesan, a thing of little or no account at the time and whose preservation at all is a matter of chance, but to us today, at any rate in the West, so much more vital and artistically valid than the other.

'The Rape', the wonderful drawing in the Musée Guimet (plate 34), is another fortunate survival: one of the host of preliminary sketches which Hokusai no doubt made when preparing the illustrations for the monumental novel which, under the name of *Shimpan Suiko Gaden* occupied no less than 90 volumes and was published over a period extending from 1807 to 1828. This is a revealing drawing in that it shows Hokusai feeling his way, first with a very rough outline and then rapid but more certain lines, though even then not without the need for *pentimenti*, a large emendation in the lower part of the drawing having been effected by pasting a piece of paper over the first draught. A comparison with the book illustration (plate 35) for which this sketch was a draught of the main figures will reveal that yet another drawing, destroyed when the block was cut, must have been prepared from Hokusai's *shita-e*, in which the lines would have been still further strengthened and organised, and the brush-strokes given that careful modulation, the swelling and dwindling which was almost a convention of Japanese brushwork for such Chinese-inspired illustrations as these.

Two further albums of drawings can be dated, one with certainty, the other by inference, to the twenties. The first, in the British Museum, contains the preparatory drawings (plates 38, 39) for a picture-book published in 1829, another book, incidentally, based on the Suikoden,[1] that interminable Chinese novel of homicide and rape which provided subject-matter to a great number of Japanese artists besides Hokusai, Kuniyoshi in particular. In the West, we do not warm to the contents of this or similar compilations, and however much they may have ministered to a craving of the, then, unwarlike Japanese male for 'blood and thunder', we are unsympathetic to this parade of inhuman heroes and their terrifying instruments of battle and torture. The callous brutality of the prints is typified by one in which a desperado is puddling the fingers of his right hand in the neck of his paramour, while in the left he is nonchalantly swinging by the hair the decapitated head of a rival. But at their best, the designs justify themselves, like the best of Salvator Rosa, by a sort of pictorial rhodomontade, with a swaggering line that matches the braggadocio of the bandits and generals. The comparison of original preparatory drawing and resultant woodcut (plate 40) is again instructive, emphasising the losses (and the gains: for the prints have their triumphs, too) that are incurred in the translation.

There is little doubt about the date of this album, but the next to be described, in the Bibliothèque Nationale in Paris, cannot be pin-pointed with such assurance. It is, in fact, a collection of drawings probably covering a number of years, for they have been pasted into an album, presumably by some admiring pupil into whose possession that had fallen. One of them (plate 42) is a study for one of the prints in the splendid Hokusai *ehon Hokusai Imagawa* (plate 43). This book is undated and the traditionally accepted date is between 1844 and 1848. Looking at it afresh, however, and guided, indeed, by the drawings in this album, I would say it too was designed in the late twenties.

The album is a collection of first thoughts for book illustrations and random jottings of all kinds (plates 44, 45) obviously designed for a book of the Suikoden kind, though I have not actually located the woodcuts that resulted from them, and their style has much in common with the drawings in the British Museum which can be dated with reasonable accuracy.

In 1819–1820, Hokusai assumed the name I-itsu, and many of the greatest prints, produced in the next twelve years, bear the signature Zen (formerly) Hokusai I-itsu. The wonderful series of landscapes—the 'Thirty-six Views of Fuji', the 'Waterfalls' and 'Bridges' and the noble prints of 'Birds and Flowers', were all designed during this period and we look with

---

[1] 'Collection of Pictures of the Heroes of Suikoden', 1829.

added interest at the drawings which correspond in time with this period of inspired designing for the colour-print. Curiously enough, few landscape drawings have survived and the screen reproduced (plate 51), which, from the retention of the name Katsushika, may be considered to have been painted soon after the change of name around 1820–1822, is as distant as can possibly be imagined from the broad style of the finest Fuji prints. Indeed, in this and in several other landscape screens and *kakemono*, Hokusai seemed hampered by a half-assimilated knowledge of Western techniques, and the solidity of foliage and houses in this view of Enoshima in juxtaposition to the vaporous washes in foreground and distance, give the painting an unreal hybridic appearance that is neither East nor West.

In the two light-heartedly painted fans (plates 52, 53), however, we find the old uninhibited bravura and intuitive flair for conveying a subject with complete freshness and at the same time giving the ink—the scumbled washes, the incisive line, the play and contrast between tone and tone—a quite abstract virtue. Plate 48, another sketch playful in subject and treatment, is masterly, the great sweeps on arm and shoulder, the lightning zig-zag strikes to denote the folds in the dress, for all their dash and daring, convincingly convey the form and movement of the masquerading badger. It is sleight-of-hand, nothing deeper, perhaps, but we cannot deny we are carried away by the performer's skill.

The two watercolour paintings of flowering gourds (plates 54, 55) are something of a different order altogether. There is nothing random or playful in the artist's approach: the drawings, in their medium, are conceived on the same serious plane as the great series of colour-prints of 'Birds and Flowers' designed at roughly the same time. They convey a high-minded veneration for nature and for the art, ancient in China and Japan, of projecting that veneration into the very drawing and composition of their transcripts from nature, whether landscape, or *kacho-e*, bird and flower, paintings. Yet the drawings are far from being sterile copies of the gourds and insects, the technique gives an interplay of textures that is solely the result of manipulation of brush and paint and the emphasis of tone follows the dictates of composition, not light and shade. Perhaps they lack the spontaneity of the sketches we think of as inimitably Hokusai, as if the voice were a little restrained by the solemnity of the occasion, but even then, there are compensations in the sincere ring of these deeper notes, only rarely heard in the master's work.

Fine drawings of this type, and with an irrefutable claim to authenticity, are those that had been mounted in *makimono* form and came into the possession of the artist Kyosai, who obtained it from Hokusai's heirs. From Kyosai, it was acquired by the great Japanophile Gonse, who gave an ecstatic description of it in Volume I of his *L'Art Japonais* published in 1883. In view of the importance of this *recueil*, which has now once again been broken up and the fragments scattered in a number of collections, it is useful to have Gonse's own account of it. It consisted of two parts: one of twelve paintings of the 'Occupations of the Twelve Months'; the other, of forty-six watercolour or ink drawings of varied subject. Gonse wrote: 'As to the forty-six water-colours of varied sizes and periods, they are of an extraordinary beauty. Never has a more skilful hand passed over paper; one cannot touch them without emotion; it is Japanese art at its greatest *éclat*, freshness, life and originality. All sorts of motives, studies of figures, of gestures, of attitudes, flowers, fruit, insects, butterflies of diapered colour, tiny animals puffed up with energy, succeed each other with the unexpected and particularised aspects of nature observed by a unique eye. Each page is a composition of genius, an accomplished fragment before which the critic is dumb; here, it is a cicada poised on a gourd or a moth flying about a branch of hydrangea; there, a rat eating a slice of water-melon or a gold-fish frolicking in a crystal vase. It is worth noting that several of these motives occur, but never identically, in the printed albums. They belong, by their execution, to the last thirty years of the artist's life, that is to say his best period. The finest in amplitude of style, the most characteristic both in feeling and in brush-strokes, are those that seem to be the most recent. There are certain studies of philosophers which are worthy to bear the signature of Rembrandt, and I say that literally. Some of the water-colours are certainly later than 1840; the earliest do not go back before 1810.'

A number of sections of this famous *makimono*, then in the possession of Felix Tikotin, were exhibited at the Arts Council's Hokusai Exhibition in 1954. Plates 55, 72 and 73 are of drawings that formed part of the scroll.

Wash-drawings of this kind, either in ink or colour, form a rather separate group (plate 49). They offer the investigator even fewer holds than the line drawings, for the method obscures the brush-line and the subjects are usually without figures (they are nearly all *kacho-e*, 'bird-and-flower' studies), so that the two features in which Hokusai's idiosyncrasies are most pronounced are absent. Monochrome wash drawings that have something in common with the scroll paintings are in the Victoria and Albert Museum and elsewhere, and one from the Museum is reproduced (plate 12). Here my feeling is that, if the drawing is indeed Hokusai's, the signature and seal are possibly a later interpolation, since this drawing, and several others in the same museum similarly signed, appear to be later than the period (ending about 1812) during which Hokusai used this form of signature.

The 'presentation' drawings mentioned earlier pose more problems of attribution than all other types. In so many of them—drawings, too, that have come down with the most respectable credentials—there is a lack of that indefinable 'touch', the confident *premier coup* that involuntarily delivers the message, almost without the volition of the artist. These drawings have a studied, thoughtful line, often of great beauty, but the suave beauty imposed by an artist who is conscious he is being watched, and who if anything accentuates the stylisation of his manner, the calligraphic quality of the line. Many of these drawings have been fervently admired, and the best have a grace and serenity for which the expression 'masterly' seems appropriate: and yet, they are the easiest of Hokusai's drawings to copy, or to imitate, since they are not the product of his first inspiration, the intuitive use of brush and ink on the impulse to realise an object, to bring it into being, on paper.

Plates 56 and 57 are from drawings of rather similar subject. The one, in the Chaikin Collection, is drawn with a line that is assured and unfaltering, the pose is easy, the dress falls into its folds naturally. The drawing in the Victoria and Albert Museum, on the other hand, superficially from the same artist, on closer inspection reveals an uncertainty in the line, the brush-tip seems to have groped its way without being sure of its destination, and the whirlpool of lines to denote the dress is meaningless. This must be a copy of a Hokusai drawing, or a pupil's attempt to draw in the manner of Hokusai. In this case the evidence is fairly conclusive, but in many other instances one is left with a doubt: Hokusai or a particularly skilled follower? The drawings reproduced in plates 58–61, 64–66 convince me, so far as any drawing of this unrevealing kind can.

Another group of drawings in a recently discovered sketch-book is diametrically opposed in treatment to the 'presentation' type. These sketches (plates 46, 63) have every appearance of being drawn *ad vivum*, the brush interpreting with lightning rapidity the artist's perception. The experienced, innate, mastery of the artist controls the darting, sweeping brush-tip and even at the white-heat of creation—in seizing a momentarily held position, or in striving for a line that will suggest actual movement—calmly imposes a formal harmony in terms of composition and accents of brush-tone. The style of the 'Old couple seated' is exactly that of a famous drawing illustrated in Fenollosa's Catalogue of the 1900 Tokyo exhibition (No. 119) which has a vivid self-portrait of Hokusai at the centre. On this sheet is a drawing of another head which, from a number of physiognomical features, seems to be identical with the old man in the newly discovered sketch-book (plate 63).

5. Hokusai's Drawings: 1839–1849

AFTER 1839, the year of Hokusai's eightieth birthday (seventy-ninth by our computation), there are greater opportunities to follow chronologically the progress of his work as it unfolds during the last decade of his life since most of the paintings and many of the drawings were dated as well as signed, or at least proudly bore the old man's age. The period contains many of his finest extant drawings, but this is partly the result of the preservation of a greater number from the last ten years of his life than from any earlier period. It would not be correct to assume a steady evolution of greater skill and feeling so that post-1839 drawings might automatically be expected to surpass those of earlier date. To my mind, his work—as might be expected in a man of his advanced years— becomes if anything more uneven, and though there are unmatchable drawings that seem to have the moving expressiveness wrung from him by experience, many others show mannerisms hardened into eccentricity, which are equally the outcome of the inflexibility of old age.

With few exceptions, the greatest colour-prints and the finest *ehon* belong to the years before 1839: and the series 'The One-hundred Poems explained by the Nurse', which appeared about 1839, signed with the newly adopted name of Manji, astonishing as they are in many ways, rarely rise to the height of the finest landscapes. Drawings intended for prints of this series but which were never cut on the wood are among the best-known of

Hokusai's ink drawings, and have given rise to some controversy. It was ambitiously intended that the series would be one of 100 prints, one for each poem of the '100 Poets': it is believed that Hokusai completed his drawings for the set, but only twenty-seven colour-prints were published, whilst one other is known only from a key-block proof. Most of the seventy-two remaining drawings have now been accounted for in collections throughout the world. A great part of them are in the Freer Gallery, where Dr. Harold P. Stern has been engaged for some years in a study of this group of drawings.

The stumbling-block to unqualified acceptance of these drawings lies in the comparative tameness and dryness of the brushwork. There is no doubt at all that the original conception behind each was Hokusai's, and that he prepared the first draughts from which the existing drawings were developed. (See, for instance, plate 71, from the first draught for one of the series.) It is undeniable that artists of Hokusai's stature did provide drawings ready for the block-cutter, but it is also generally agreed that publishers sometimes employed 'copyists' whose function it was to prepare for the block-cutter sketches and other drawings unsuitable in the form presented by the original designer. The issue in regard to the drawings for the 'One-hundred Poems' is simply this: were they drawn by Hokusai, or by an artist in the publisher's studio working from Hokusai's first draughts?

Plates 68–70 are from the series. They are all sufficiently full of Hokusai's mannerisms at this time—easily checked against the colour-prints that *were* published: but I personally find it difficult to believe that Hokusai dabbed in the background of misty river and bridge in plate 70; or dotted the foliage in plate 68; or neatly filled in the leggings of the porters in plate 69. In every case, the brushwork is too mechanical, too menially subservient to the requirements of the block-cutter; it is the work of a patient and able copyist making the way plain for the cutter, but hardly what we would expect from a man of Hokusai's artistry and temperament.

I am bound to admit the counter-evidence, and also that I am in a minority in believing them to be a copyist's work. The inscriptions are fairly certainly in Hokusai's calligraphy (comparison can be made with a further example in plate 87). This is inconclusive in itself since Hokusai could have written the inscriptions in the cartouches but still not have been responsible for the drawings—it must be remembered that the inscription on painting or print was of real importance, and an astute publisher (as Eijudo was) might well have insisted on Hokusai's inscribing poems and signature.

Again, it is asked, if these are the copies for the block-cutter, what of Hokusai's original sketches? Only a few have survived.[1] But is the destruction of first drafts in any way different from what we have deduced of normal practice? We have to remind ourselves that among the producers of Ukiyo-e prints there was no especial virtue in the first design —all that really mattered was the ultimate result, the finished colour-print, in which the parts played by copyist, block-cutter and printer were almost as important as the

---

[1] By the kindness of Madame Berès, I am able to illustrate what is obviously the first draft, replete with *pentimenti*, of the design for the print illustrating the poem by Ariwara no Narihira (plate 71). The figures, some added on the *pentimenti*, are carefully drawn, but the brush line is alive, and incontestably Hokusai's: the landscape and bridge are clearly first thoughts in an impetuous line that is trying to keep pace with the artist's mental conception of the composition. It would be instructive to compare this rough draft with the finished drawing prepared for the block-cutter, but in this case, the colour-print was produced and the drawing destroyed when the block was cut.

designer's. It is quite conceivable that, having served their purpose as the basis for the colour-prints, the *shita-e*, the first sketches, were destroyed, possibly with Hokusai's consent. He, too, may have seen his drawings as the first in a chain of operations leading up to the ultimate print.

Proof one way or another is not likely to be produced, but my own view is that, interesting as these drawings may be, they lack the spontaneity and sparkle of the finest drawings.

The next group of drawings illustrate the antithesis both to the 'presentation' type and to those provided for the block-cutter. The two sheets of drawings of the 'Sparrow Dance' (plates 72, 73) are captivating and amusing, and rely greatly on the bold brushwork, the contrasts between the heavy, moist black of the 'wings' of the performers and the almost dry brush-strokes outlining the limbs and marking, with a swift series of radial lines, the forms of the straw hats. The spirited action in the line of figures is syncopated by the brilliant changes in ink-tone and brush-stroke.

The Louvre drawing of a seated woman (plate 74) has a similar warmth of tone in the ink but an even more daring sweep of line. But forceful and massive as the strokes may be, they do not obscure the artist's primary object, the portrayal of a seated woman, and the splendour of his attack is seen in such a detail as the bold curve indicating the thigh and knee of the left leg turned under the woman, and the deft swing of lines of the hood, which both model the head and emphasise the downward drag of the heavy material of the hood. The Freer drawing of the 'Cloth Merchant' and the 'Sleeping Girl' in the Chaikin Collection (plates 75, 80) have obvious affinities with the Louvre drawing.

It is not possible to date the drawings reproduced in plates 50 and 71 but they appear to be late works and a development from the kind of drawing just mentioned. Indeed, the 'Woodman' (plate 81) might be thought to be the ultimate, the *ne plus ultra*, of swift, intuitive painting of this order; it is undoubtedly a most powerful and satisfying drawing, and clearly the work of a master.

Another distinguished work in the Freer Gallery, dated 1839, is a *makimono*, a long laterally unfolding scroll, of a kind only rarely affected by Hokusai. Among artists of the Shijo, naturalistic, school, it was a much commoner vehicle, the long unwinding surface being used for a succession of separate drawings of diverse subjects, selected solely, it would seem, for the opportunity they afforded of displaying brushwork. Hokusai's scroll (plate 82) is similar in intent, with a choice of subjects ranging from fish-heads to fox-priests, and allowing him free scope to demonstrate his virtuosity.

I come now to another of those albums that have survived from varying periods of Hokusai's career, providing some generally accepted anchorages for voyagers along a coastline about which cartographers differ. The *Nisshin Joma*, 'Daily Exorcisms', is one of the best known of these albums, partly on account of the strange motive behind the drawings, and partly because the Kokka Company published a large selection from it in 1906. During a period commencing about 1842, Hokusai began the practice of drawing each day a *shishi*, a 'Chinese Lion', as a talisman to ward off evil. Each was dated, and, according to tradition, was thrown away by the artist at the end of the day. But his daughter Oei, who looked after him in his old age, preserved a large number, and later gave them to a Mr. Shinsuke Miyamoto, who had been promised a drawing by Hokusai for the hospitality he had shown the old artist at some earlier period. The story of the making of this gift, a story handed down to the son of Shinsuke, Mr. Chu Miyamoto, who owned the album when the Kokka publication appeared in 1906, is clearly reliable and corroborated by inscriptions in Hokusai's own unmistakable hand in the album itself. We have therefore, in the drawings reproduced in plates 76–79, undoubted specimens from the artist's brush during the years 1842–1843, still in the possession of a descendant of the original recipient.

Although they began as simple drawings of the *shishi*, that fabulous beast described in an old saying as 'the lion, the king of beasts who commands all lower creation and destroys evil spirits', quite soon Hokusai's inventive and playful approach created entirely new motifs, and men and boys in the lion-mask adopted for the *shishi-mai*, the 'Lion Dance', enrich the thematic material and give Hokusai scope for some of his happiest compositions.

The album of sketches belonging to Mr. Shozaburo Watanabe, known as 'Life in the Eastern Capital', is placed in this decade by Ichitaro Kondo[1] but the tight line and the careful painting generally in these drawings have more in common with the 'One-hundred Poems' than the drawings just discussed. The 'Life in the Eastern Capital' drawings (plates 83, 84) repeat the eternal theme of the 'Day and Night' album, but are carefully worked out, with a neat finish and a studied line that is utterly opposed to the licence and verve of the earlier set. Here again, if the drawings are indeed from the master's hand, and not from that of a talented pupil working from Hokusai's first drafts, we must assume a commission, a working to instructions, perhaps with an eye to eventual publication as a woodblock *ehon*, and this need to conform has inhibited some of those qualities which are the stamp of the most characteristic Hokusai drawings.

Another album of about this period is in the Harari Collection. This is a collection of diverse drawings of *kakemono* dimensions (plates 85–90) which may well have been put together by a pupil, since they bear signs of having been produced over a number of years, though all within the final phase of the artist's life. Eight of the drawings are of unidentifiable warriors (plates 85–87) of the strangely accoutred and frighteningly weaponed type that teem in certain books of the mid-thirties—*Ehon Sakigake* and *Ehon Mushi Abumi*, for example. These drawings, however, were not intended for illustration to books; they are on too big a scale altogether, and give the impression of being the first drafts for the panels of a screen. This is rather confirmed by two of the drawings that have an identical subject, one being the first rough undeveloped outline, the other the next stage in the development, with parts worked out in complete detail and textual notes added concerning colour and treatment generally (plate 87). These notes can only refer to some final painting in a yet more complete, coloured, form; and in view of the elaborateness of the preliminary stages, it is reasonable to surmise that the ultimate version was to be a work of some moment, and a screen immediately comes to mind.

---

[1] *Katsushika Hokusai*, Kodansha Library of Japanese Art No. 1.

As it will throw light on Hokusai's methods (a practical demonstration of what he advised in his primer *Ehon Saishiki Tsu*, published in 1848), a translation of the long inscription on his drawings follows: 'On the face use a thin layer of *benigara* (red oxide of iron) with a wash of *taisha* (red ochre or burnt sienna). The outline of the face is drawn with a double application of *benigara*. Then first tint the details of the face with a slightly thicker colour and graduate this out over the whole face. The eye-shadows are to be coloured light grey, the eyeballs with *benigara-zumi* (ink with *benigara*), and the pupils of the eyes with *konzumi* (Chinese dark black ink). The moustache is to be shaped with *benigara-zumi*, and the hairs drawn one by one with the brush.'

The inscription is thought to be in Hokusai's hand, and can be compared with other examples of his calligraphy in plates 68–70. What of the final version, to which the two drawings in the Harari album were preparatory? So far, I have been unable to locate any painting, screen or otherwise, based on this drawing (or of the other six warriors, since they are likely to have been developed in the same way), but this is hardly surprising. Many major works of art have perished in earthquake, fire, flood and air attack in Japan during the last hundred years, most of them before photographic or even wood-block records of them had been made. Others lie in collections that have never been publicly exhibited. But even if the screen were to be discovered, it might easily prove to have been painted by pupils of Hokusai: the inscription on the drawing seems to have been added for guidance, and one would hardly imagine that Hokusai would need to write such *aides-memoire* to himself.

The warriors, although comprising half the drawings in the album, are by no means the chief attraction. Indeed, as has been mentioned above, they belong to a class that has never given rise to anything like the enthusiasm with which it was acclaimed in its day by the Japanese themselves, perhaps because it appealed to a resurgent martial spirit, or to patriotic feelings that we cannot share. The remaining drawings are varied and exceptionally interesting.

Perhaps the finest is the mountain landscape (plate 89). This has a serenity and sublimity attained to by only few of the master's works. The 'Red Fuji' comes to mind at once because of a similarity of effect, however different the landscape. The print is a stylised representation of Fuji, epitomising the awe in which the Peerless Mountain is held in Japan. The drawing is an evocation of peaks conceived in a mind haunted by Chinese painting, they are veritably the 'Mountains of the Heart' that inspire so much of Chinese art. Yet nobody familiar with Oriental painting could mistake this drawing of impossible peaks towering over snow-bound cottages for a Chinese painting. The Chinese elements have been translated into Japanese and, in some indefinable way, the romantic and emotive appeal heightened in the process.

As I have already mentioned, the drawings belong to the artist's maturity. In several instances there are obvious parallels to paintings exhibited in the great Tokyo Exhibition of 1900, paintings either dated in the last decade of the artist's life, or attributable to that period. A drawing of a 'Blue Heron Perched on a Stump' in the album is strongly reminiscent in pose and treatment of a painting dated 1847 reproduced in the Catalogue of the

1900 Exhibition (No. 211), and the drawing might well be considered a preliminary study for the painting. Another drawing in the album is a fully worked out watercolour of a 'Fisherman with Net', in a style that is unmistakably of Hokusai's last years (plate 90). This bears the clearest affinity—in the method of watercolouring, in the heavy modelling in very deep reds—with the painting of a woodcutter also reproduced in the 1900 Catalogue (No. 219), and now in the Freer Gallery (plate 91). The Freer painting is signed by Hokusai in the last year of his life (aged ninety: eighty-nine by our computation) in 1849. The remaining drawings in this outstanding album are of a 'Dragon'; a 'Group of Fish'; a 'Skeleton with Lantern' (very typical of the naïve macabre that often occurs in Hokusai's work); a 'Study of Pine-trees' (plate 88); and 'Kintaro and Yama-Uba struggling with a Giant Carp'. All have the stamp, in varying degrees of intensity, of the marvellous old man's personality. All speak with his unmistakable voice.

6. Drawings by Hokusai's Followers: Taito, Hokkei and Hokuba

ALTHOUGH there is general agreement that only a proportion of the drawings attributed to Hokusai are actually by him, little attention has so far been given to the artists who were capable of causing the confusion, though their own work must obviously be of some merit to have been accepted as Hokusai's. The tendency has been to ignore everything that failed to pass a test of authentication—a test, as I conveyed earlier, that varies from one individual to another, and for which no infallible Geiger-counter is likely to be invented. Yet in applying this test, it would obviously narrow the field of possibilities if we have a clear conception of the styles and the capabilities of those artists whose work resembled Hokusai's most closely. A study of the engraved work of such pupils as Taito II, Hokkei, Yanagawa Shigenobu and Isai and of the small number of drawings and paintings signed, or otherwise known to be by these artists, not only brings some definition to the style of these men, but also provides criteria by which certain unsigned drawings can be detached from the vast Hokusai corpus and given, with more certainty, to pupils and followers. Hokuba's paintings are well-known and he is an accepted master in his own right, but very few *shita-e* as distinct from *kakemono* paintings are known, and it is instructive to study a number of his less finished brush-drawings alongside comparable works of Hokusai of the same periods.

Genryusai Taito is, I consider, the leading suspect for a great many of the drawings that pass as Hokusai's, and he merits more attention than he has been given in the past. His story is that of an artist who followed Hokusai so closely that he has been lost in that master's shadow. His finest books have repeatedly been, and still are, given to Hokusai, by his own countrymen as much as by foreigners. His picture book of flowers and birds, the *Kacho Gaden*, published as late as 1848–1849, was actually renamed *Hokusai Kacho Gaden* in later editions, though Hokusai had no hand in it at all; until quite recently, the book of illustrated comic poems, *Nihon Meibutsu Gasen Kyoka Shu*, was praised as Hokusai's (even Vignier, in his Paris sale catalogues, usually so reliable, fell into this error); and Mizutani, a sound investigator, reproduces as Hokusai's, in his study of illustrated novels,[1] one of the colour-prints in Part III of *Ehon Saiyuki* (the novel known to us, from Waley's translation, under the title of *Monkey*), the illustrations to which were provided by Taito some fourteen or fifteen years after Hokusai had ceased to use the name Taito. The colour-print of 'The Carp', the best-known of all his works, is still invariably credited to Hokusai; and even in 1962, a writer in the *British Museum Quarterly* permits himself to doubt whether Taito II ever did exist at all![2]

It is a case, too, of an artist being his own worst enemy as regards posterity, for Taito signed his finest prints not with his own name, but with the forged signature of I-itsu, one of Hokusai's names. One set of birds and flowers with this forged signature has been identified with certainty as Taito's because they were based on designs used also in the *Kacho Gaden* already mentioned, but I believe there are many other prints, equally fine, that still pass as Hokusai's, adding little, possibly, to that great artist's stature, but which, recognised as the follower's, would elevate Taito to a much higher place in our esteem.

His real name was Kameya Saburo, but like most Japanese artists, he employed a number of art-names, Toenro Hokusen, Katsushika Taito, Genryusai Taito and, less frequently, Doteisha, Shozan, Beikasai and Baikasanjin. Whether or not he used the name Taigaku will be discussed later.

The scanty biographical details that have come down to us are far from complimentary. His other profession seems to have been that of pandar, for he owned one of the *hikite-ya*, 'guide tea-houses', which was a polite name for a house of assignation in the Yoshiwara or courtesan quarter, and later, when he had moved from Edo to Osaka, he earned the nickname 'Dog Hokusai' for forging his master's signature on his own prints.

It is not known when he first enrolled himself as a pupil of Hokusai, but it must have been at a date prior to the publication in 1815 of Vol. II of Hokusai's *Manga*—in which the assistance of Toenro Hokusen is specifically recorded. In 1819 Hokusai bestowed upon him the name Taito, which he had, from 1811, been using himself, with authority to use the family art-name of Katsushika. The picture-book *Nijushi-ko Zue* ('Twenty-four examples of Filial Piety in Pictures') appeared under the signature of Katsushika Taito in the same year, 1819, a seal that follows the signature reading Toenro Katsushika To Hokusen and placing beyond any doubt the identity of Taito II with Hokusen and the date of the transfer of the name. It might be assumed that after that date anything appearing under the name of Taito is the work of the pupil, but there is at least one curious exception, the painting of the 'Cormorant Fishers' to be discussed shortly.

The development of Taito's style can be followed through the numerous books for which

---

[1] *Kohan Shogetsu Soga Shi*, 1935.
[2] *British Museum Quarterly*, vol. xxv, 1962: D. B. Waterhouse 'Twelve Japanese Prints'.

he provided illustration. As his work has so often been confounded with Hokusai's, it may be as well to establish his claim to the following:

Nijushi-ko Zue, 'Twenty-four Examples of Filial Piety in Pictures', 1819.

Kyoka Shinsen Kacho Fugetsu Shu, 'Collection of Newly-composed Poems on Birds, Flowers, Wind and Moon': landscapes by Taito, figures by Hokusai, 1824.

Banshoku Zuko 'Designs for All Artisans', five volumes between 1827 and 1850.

Ehon Fukushu Senjo no Matsu, 'The Pine Tree 1000 *Jo* High, a Story of Vengeance', 1828.

Nihon Meibutsu Gasen Kyoka Shu, 'Collection of Comic Poems on Noted Products of Japan', *circa* 1832.

Ehon Saiyuki, 'The illustrated Record of the Western Trip' Third and Fourth parts illustrated by Taito 1833 and 1835.

Eiyu Zue, 'Pictures of Heroes', *circa* 1838.

Jingo Kogo Sankan Zue, 'Pictorial Account of the Empress Jingo in Korea', 1840.

Ehon Tsuzoku Sangoku-shi 'Illustrated Popular Edition of "History of the Three Countries"', Parts 6, 7 and 8, 1840 and 1841.

Harimaze han, 'The Printed Miscellany for Pasting', *circa* 1843.

Ehon Yanagi-taru, 'The Picture Book of the Cask of Willow' (a book of verses) Series 7 and 10, 1844 and 1846 (and possibly others in the series).

Kacho Gaden, 'Pictures of Flowers and Birds', 1848 and 1849.

Judging by the designs in these books—a great number spread over thirty years—one is forced to the conclusion that of all his pupils Taito most closely approached the style of the master, or perhaps one should say, the styles of the master during a certain period, say 1815 to 1830. Associated with Hokusai in the production of at least two of the *Manga* volumes, he no doubt had unprecedented opportunities for studying Hokusai's method, probably made a practice of copying studies with a view to emulating his style—a number of drawings exist which seem to be of this kind—and in the end so thoroughly assimilated, at least superficially, Hokusai's brush style that it is small wonder that his drawings have been confused with his master's. His was a smaller talent than Hokusai's, of course. In his work, there is not the continual unfolding of new vistas that we experience in going through any chronological selection of Hokusai's work, where the changes in style and matter are so remarkable that the Fuji landscapes of the 1830s and the Sumidagawa book-designs of twenty-five years earlier could be the work of two different individuals. Taito's *Kacho Gaden* of 1848–1849 has much to remind us of the early *Manga* volumes in which he had had a hand more than thirty years earlier, and there is little in the *Eiyu Zue* of 1838 that is not already present in the *Nijushi-ko Zue* of 1819. But having admitted that minor and limited talent, it has also to be conceded that he was a very fair copyist of his master, and occasionally, as in the *Ehon Saiyuki*, produced some really striking designs, whilst in the *Nihon Meibutsu* book of verses he proved his ability in a *genre* that few besides Hokusai had successfully exploited. Above all, I think, he had more ability with the brush than most of his contemporaries.

In an investigation such as this, signed drawings by the followers of Hokusai are of first importance. Such drawings are extremely uncommon, but they can, as a rule, be accepted as authentic. The 'traffic' in drawings has not extended to men who based their style on Hokusai's: it was just as easy, and far more profitable, to forge the signature of Hokusai as that of any lesser man.

The identification of a body of drawings in the Victoria and Albert Museum as Taito's, with certainty in some cases, and with strong probability in others, gives me an unparalleled opportunity to bring forward a number of the drawings of this artist for direct comparison with Hokusai's own work. Until now, the Victoria and Albert Museum drawings have been loosely catalogued as Hokusai's, but one album of sketches bears the title, written by a former Japanese owner, *Genryusai Taito Zatsuga*, 'Miscellaneous Drawings by Genryusai Taito'; others are sealed Hokusen; others are studies for woodblock prints known to be by Taito. The drawings have been mounted and bound in albums to which it is hardly accurate to attach the name of 'sketch-books'. One of the albums bears the name of a late Ukiyo-e artist of the Utagawa school, Itteisai Yoshiki, who was presumably the owner and perhaps the collector of the assortment of drawings and progress proofs of prints mounted in the albums.

Most of my illustrations of Taito's work are from this source. First however, in point of time, should be considered the painting in the Hakone Museum in Japan, ascribed by the authorities there to Hokusai (plate 94). The poem inscribed on the *kakemono* is a *haiku* on cormorant fishing by Tani Sogai, an Edo poet, who signed his poem Tama-ike (an alternative name from the place where he lived) adding 'Old man of 87'. Now Tani Sogai died at the (Japanese) age of ninety in 1823, and thus this painting, signed Katsushika Taito, must have been executed in 1820, the year following that in which Hokusai had given up the use of the name Taito.[1] The seal, Fujiyama, is one Hokusai used: but it was not unknown for a master to allow a pupil the use of a seal: nor for someone to add a seal in after years with a view to placing the authenticity of a painting beyond doubt. In fact, a strong case could be made for this painting being by the pupil, Taito, except that the style is so unmistakably Hokusai's, and it is difficult to believe that Taito could have so successfully imitated his master at this period. But later exploits of Taito II must put us on our guard, and the Hakone painting is now, for me, faintly open to suspicion.

The drawing of a duck and a peasant with a mattock over his shoulder (plate 92) is sealed Hokusen. The former ascription to Hokusai is understandable; the seal serves to remind us how dangerously close the style of a pupil could approach to the master's. The next two—the girl walking with closed umbrella, and the seated girl with a pipe in front of her (plates 95, 96) all come from the book of sketches labelled *Genryusai Taito Zatsuga*. They have something of the summary skill of Hokusai, of his expressive, flowing and rhythmic line. The sketches of figures, especially the men and women hauling on

---

[1] Information kindly supplied by Dr. Richard Lane.

ropes (plate 99) have just that impress of reality, that facility for hitting off movement in a few sure touches, that we admire in a Hokusai drawing. The girl with a *samisen* (plate 93) is very reminiscent of a drawing in the Freer Gallery, attributed to Hokusai. This is perhaps an instance, far from isolated, of Taito copying a drawing by Hokusai, presumably without intent to deceive, for it is doubtful if drawings by Hokusai were in demand during or shortly after his lifetime as they have become since. Another of the drawings (plate 98) in the Victoria and Albert Museum sketch-book is probably a pre-liminary study for the well-known print (plate 97) of a 'Courtesan Promenading'. This appeared in the *Harimaze han* of 1843 and has often been ascribed to Hokusai in common with all the best things of this unjustly overlooked pupil.

A sketch-book in the Honolulu Academy of Arts is full of drawings that can be traced to a number of Hokusai's picture-books, and also to Taito's *Ehon Saiyuki*. They lack the qualities of original spontaneous sketches and are evident copies, no doubt intended to be passed off as Hokusai's and so copied from a variety of his books—or what were thought to be Hokusai's books: the *Saiyuki* was almost certainly mistaken by the copyist (as it has been by so many others) for Hokusai's. An enlarged detail is given of one of the pages of this album of sketches to illustrate the difference between the line of a freely drawn original sketch and of a copy, where the brush halts and starts, and has no life, no verve (plate 100).

A subsidiary problem that has arisen out of a study of the Victoria and Albert Museum drawings is the identity of the artist using the name of Taigaku. It has generally been held that Taigaku was another name used by Taito, but there seems little proof of this. The earliest dated appearance of the name seems to be in an erotic book *Wago shu*, 'All in Harmony', dated, according to Shibui, 1826.[1] The name also appears on a number of prints in the *Harimaze han* of about 1843 already referred to, sometimes on the same sheet with other designs signed Taito. (*Harimaze* were sheets on which pictures of different shapes and sizes were printed, the intention being that the pictures should be cut out and pasted on to screens, *fusuma* and the like. *Harimaze han*, an album of such sheets, and including some of Taito's best-known prints, the often-reproduced 'Carp' and the 'Courtesan Promenading' (plate 97) especially, is almost unknown now in its complete state.) The fact of two signatures appearing together in this way seems to in-dicate two artists, since although it was not uncommon for an artist to use two or more different signatures in the same book, he was unlikely to use two names with a common derivation. On the other hand, it is recorded that on one print the name Taigaku is followed by a seal Hokusen (the first art-name of Taito), and a *surimono* in the Victoria and Albert Museum of a tobacco-box with *netsuke* in the form of a compass attached, is actually signed Hokusen Taigaku. Both these instances might be thought to identify Taigaku with Taito, but the use of the name Hokusen may indicate that Taigaku was a pupil of Taito and that the name Hokusen had been passed on to him. The drawings signed or sealed Taigaku, of which there are a number in the Victoria and Albert Museum albums, are so similar in style to those of Taito with which they are bound that one is tempted to accept the generally held view that the two names were used by the one man,

[1] *Estampes Erotiques Primitives du Japan.* 1926.

but it may, after all, be just another case of a pupil's work having a remarkable similarity to his master's, and of the collector having confounded the work of the two men.

The two drawings of a man heaving a mortar, or *usu*, out of the snow are worth considering (plates 101, 102). One of them is signed Taigaku, and this signature appears on a colour-print obviously based on the drawing. The second drawing reproduced may represent the artist's own, or another's, variation, but yet another version is known, a finished drawing in the British Museum—signed Hokusai! Furthermore a *kakemono* signed Hokusai Taito, reproduced in the Bing Sale Catalogue (No. 925) is so similar that, if indeed by Hokusai, it probably formed the inspiration of Taigaku's and all the succeeding versions. Incidentally, the print of this subject is sealed with the 'swastika' or *Manji* seal employed by Hokusai later in his life. There is no record of Hokusai's having bequeathed this name.

I turn now to another of the suspects, Hokkei. He was a more independent artist than Taito, and though he learned much in his early years from Hokusai, being, like Taito, a collaborator in the *Manga* volumes of 1815, his own work soon took on a recognisably individual cast. Even of a book like his *Hokkei Manga*, frankly borrowing from Hokusai, one might say that it was more conceived in the spirit of Hokusai than executed in his style. The bulk of Hokkei's work was in *surimono*, the ingeniously composed and exquisitely printed commemorative or greetings prints, and in the somewhat kindred illustrations to books of occasional verse. Unlike Hokusai or Taito, he had little to do with the illustration of novels: perhaps the sustained, plodding industry necessary to see one through five, ten or more volumes, was lacking. The fine set of landscapes from his designs, the 'Provinces' set, is remarkable more for the detailed rendering of incident than the grasp of composition that characterises Hokusai's 'Fuji' set. We would expect, therefore, that his brush-drawings would differ widely from Hokusai's, and judging by the evidence of the few that are known, there should be little cause to confuse his brush-drawings with those of Hokusai.

In the case of Hokkei, as of Taito, my chief source of material is the Victoria and Albert Museum. One book of mounted sketches there appears to be entirely Hokkei's work. Several of these drawings are clearly studies for prints (especially the 'Provinces' set already mentioned); one is signed Hokkei; mounted in with the drawings is an ink-proof of one of his *surimono;* and the cover of the book bears the seal Kiko, one of Hokkei's art-names. Two drawings are reproduced from this album (plates 103, 105) and point to the distinguishing traits of Hokkei's brush-drawing. He has a nervous, hesitant, less assured line that could not possibly be confused with other drawings reproduced here, and normally employs a finer brush than either Hokusai and Taito, perhaps from the habit of miniature painting imposed upon him by the demands of the *surimono*. He also had the habit, like a number of other Japanese artists, of indicating corrections and additions to his drawings in a red pigment, a practice for which Hokusai rarely found need, or which he disdained. The fine signed drawing of a crow (plate 106) shows, however, an entirely different technique, a daring bravura and a clever use of the dry brush to suggest plumage, quite at variance with his normal style. Yet this, one senses, is something of an exception and the elaborate signature and seal confirm that impression. The drawings in the album in the Victoria and Albert Museum provide an excellent guide to Hokkei's sketches, and with their aid it should not be difficult to detect drawings by Hokkei when, as is almost inevitable, they appear under Hokusai's name.

Hokuba's earliest work in book form appeared in 1798, and he was certainly one of Hokusai's earliest pupils. Moreover, born in 1770, he lived until 1844 and though there is no evidence of any close association with Hokusai after his period of tutelage, his many illustrations to novels and his *surimono* retained characteristics which link him to the Hokusai school. In his paintings, however, he is less obviously the pupil of his master. Morrison[1] speaks of the high regard the Japanese have for his painting, the respect for his 'independence of view and more classic technique' which single him out from all other Hokusai pupils. The knowledge that he had had his early training in the academic Kano school might be thought to have swayed their judgement, but there is no other pupil, apart from Taito II, whose *kakemono* approach in quality the finest of Hokusai's. In fact, Hokuba developed a strain that was of a different character altogether from the later Hokusai, and his *kakemono* have a refinement and delicate touch that reminds one more of Eishi than Hokusai. But Hokusai, even after the Sori period, when his manner had more in common with Eishi and other Ukiyo-e artists, could also on occasion adopt a softer and gentler guise, and at such times the finished works of the two painters are more liable to be confused.

However, Hokuba's drawings—the few that are known—are easily distinguishable from Hokusai's. The lovely and expressive drawing of a girl holding her battered umbrella in the snow (plate 107), reminds one perhaps of the early *bijin-ga* of Hokusai under the name of Sori (plates 2, 5), but that is simply testimony to Hokuba's upbringing, and there are details—the line of the right leg and foot for example—that, were the drawing unsigned, would preclude any possibility of ascription to Hokusai.

The other two drawings reproduced (plates 108, 109) are from an album which, before it was broken up, bore an old inscription *Hokuba Hikishita*, and there seems no reason to doubt that the drawings are rough sketches by Hokuba. They are quick notes of groups and single figures, alive and descriptive, but lacking the mastery in the medium exhibited by Hokusai in similar rapid jottings. It may seem unfair to judge Hokuba's skill as a draughtsman on what are admittedly the roughest of sketches in one album, but it is in such off-guard moments that an artist 'speaks with his own voice'. Normally, Hokuba has the most cultured accent and watches his words carefully, but here the Edokko argot slips out. One would like to compare other free drawings by Hokuba, but it is surprisingly hard to locate any that are even traditionally ascribed to him, although there are of course plenty of *kakemono* and slighter works mounted as *kakemono*.

I HAVE dealt here very briefly with the drawings of only three of Hokusai's followers, Taito II, Hokkei and Hokuba. There were many other artists who, even if they were not actually pupils, declared themselves followers of Hokusai by using names derived from the

---

[1] *The Painters of Japan*, vol. II, 1911.

master's, and of these a few at least must have been capable of producing drawings of some calibre, with the imprint of the school. Yet only very rarely do we come across signed works by them, and as a consequence no sufficient body of drawings exists by which the style of each can be known and their hand recognised when a signature is lacking. In this book, the drawings of Hokusai illustrated are in many instances beyond dispute and the remainder have been ascribed on the strength of style, traditional acceptance, provenance; many others, equally widely accepted, could be cited. There remains, however, a vast number that lie on the fringe of acceptance, drawings which have evident kinship with Hokusai but which fail to be wholly convincing. It is among these, I feel sure, that the masterpieces of the minor artists are to be found, and if by patient and disinterested research some stronger notion of the style and scope of each could be established, the means would exist to begin the task of purging the mass of so-called Hokusai drawings of those which are by other hands.

PLATES

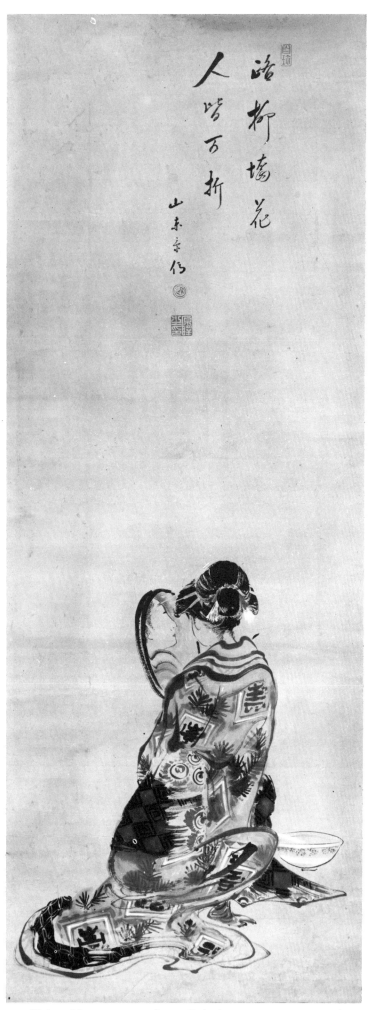

路柳墻花
人踏万折
山东东作

1. Girl making up at a mirror. Painting on paper. 53×20 in.
Hakone Museum, Japan.

2. An effeminate fop. 20×8½ in. *Freer Gallery of Art, Washington.*

3. Daikoku and Ebisu as New Year Performers. 7 × 18 in.
Freer Gallery of Art, Washington.

4. The Six Master Poets. $12\frac{3}{4} \times 22\frac{3}{16}$ in. *Freer Gallery of Art, Washington.*

5. Courtesan strolling under a full moon, verse by Santo Kyoden. $57\frac{7}{8} \times 16$ in. *Ralph Harari Collection, London.*
6. Branch of flowering plum. 46×14 in. *Ralph Harari Collection, London.*

7. Woman dressing her hair. $10\frac{1}{8} \times 6\frac{1}{2}$ in. *Metropolitan Museum of Art, New York.*
Gift in memory of Charles Stewart Smith, 1915.

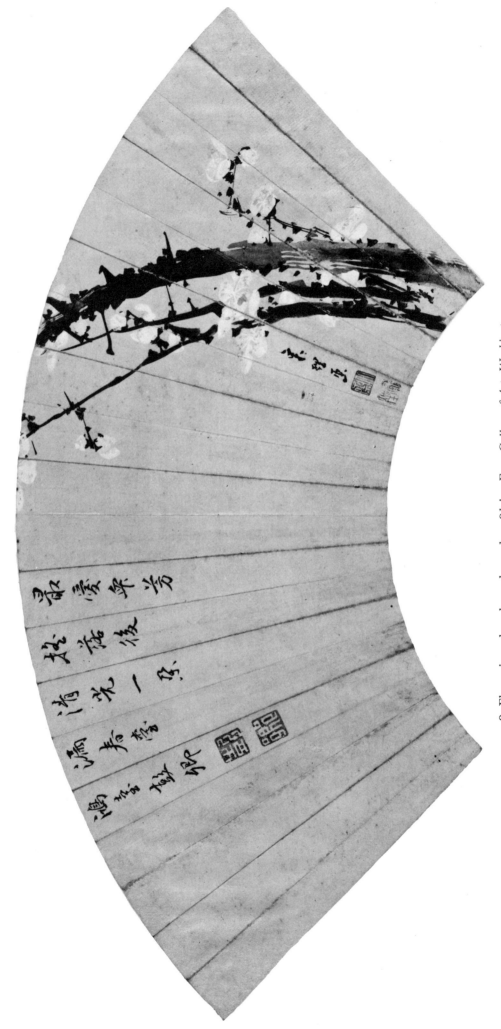

8. Flowering plum branches. $7\frac{1}{8} \times 18\frac{1}{8}$ in. *Freer Gallery of Art, Washington.*

9. Landscape. 11 ×23½ in. *Freer Gallery of Art, Washington.*

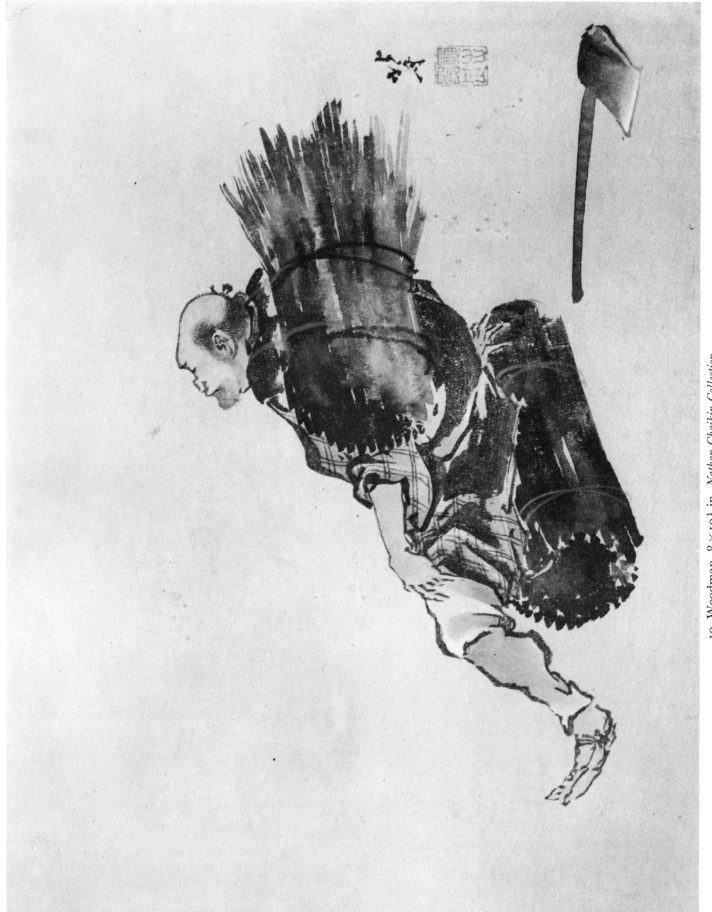

10. Woodman. 8 × 10½ in. *Nathan Chaikin Collection.*

11. Crow flying against the sun. $9\frac{3}{8} \times 11\frac{3}{4}$ in. *Nathan Chaikin Collection.*

12. Wagtail and reed. $11\frac{1}{4} \times 15$ in. *Victoria and Albert Museum, London.*

13. Pheasant in the snow. Possibly a study for the print in the *Shashin Gafu*, an album datable to 1814. 11 ×18 in. *Private collection, Italy.*

14. Acrobat performing with swords before a crowd. *Metropolitan Museum of Art, New York.*
Gift in memory of Charles Stewart Smith, 1914.

15. Posting-station beside a river. $9\frac{1}{4} \times 13$ in. Preparatory drawing for one of the illustrations to Rokujuen's
novel *Hida-no-takumi*, "The Craftsman of Hida", 1808. *Metropolitan Museum of Art, New York.*
Gift in memory of Charles Stewart Smith, 1914.

16. Tile-makers working by their kilns. $15 \times 11\frac{1}{2}$ in. *Metropolitan Museum of Art, New York.
Gift in memory of Charles Stewart Smith, 1914.*

17. Porters at a quayside. From the "Occupations" album, 1811. 11 × 15 in. *Ralph Harari Collection, London.*

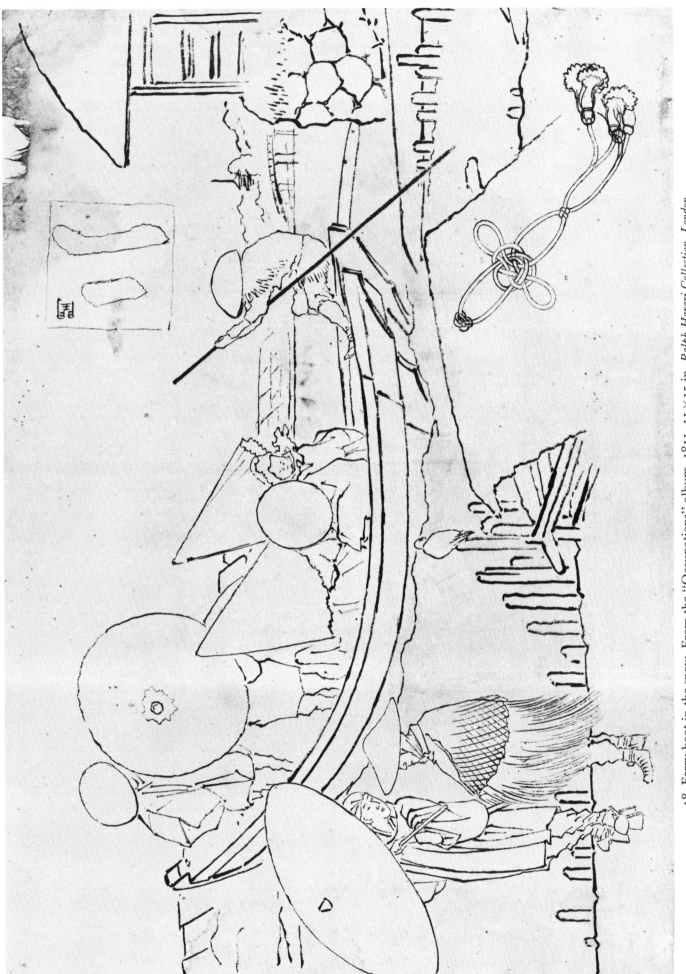

18. Ferry-boat in the snow. From the "Occupations" album, 1811. 11 × 15 in. *Ralph Harari Collection, London.*

19. Festival lantern makers. From the "Occupations" album, 1811. 11 × 15 in. *Ralph Harari Collection, London.*

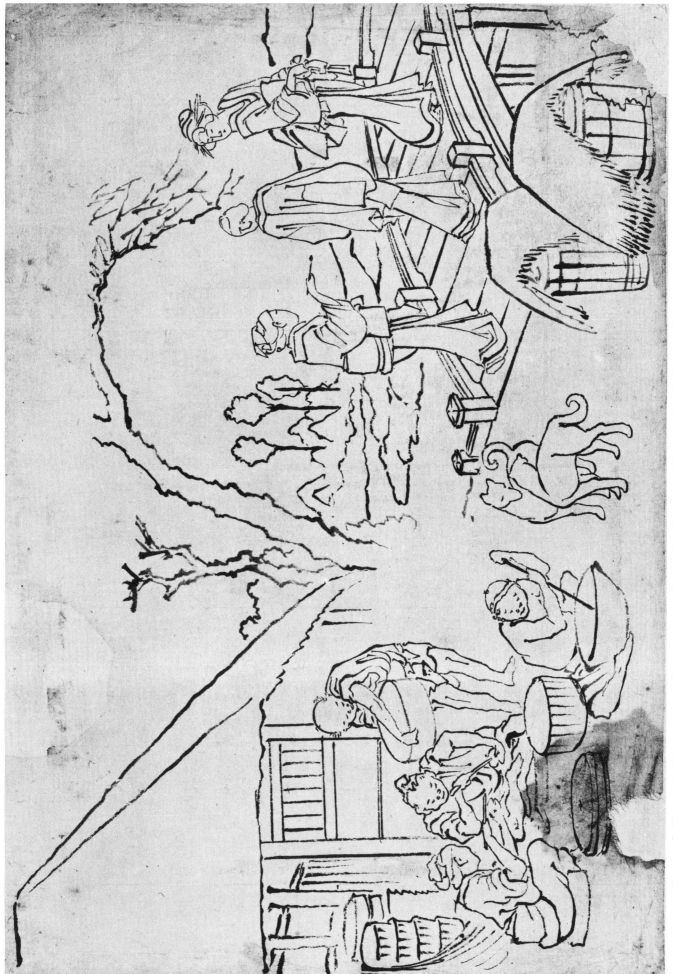

20. Group of villagers beside a cottage, others crossing a footbridge. From the "Occupations" album, 1811. 11 × 15 in. *Ralph Harari Collection, London.*

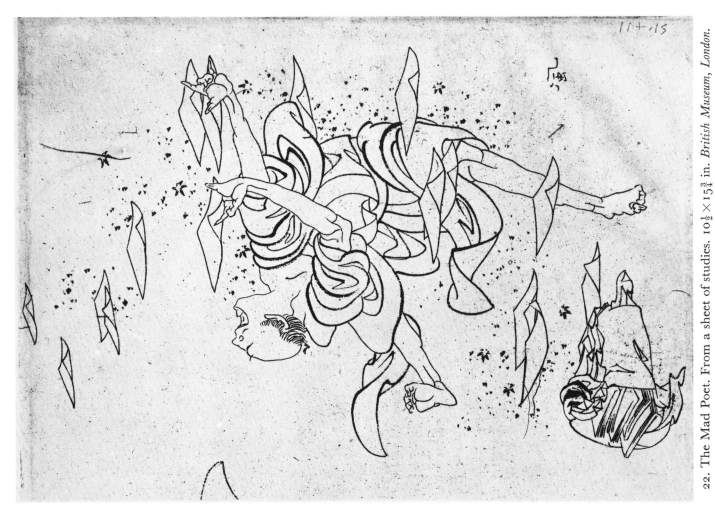

22. The Mad Poet. From a sheet of studies. $10\frac{1}{2} \times 15\frac{3}{4}$ in. *British Museum, London.*

21. The Mad Poet. From a sheet of studies. $7\frac{7}{8} \times 15\frac{7}{8}$ in. *Huguette Berès, Paris.*

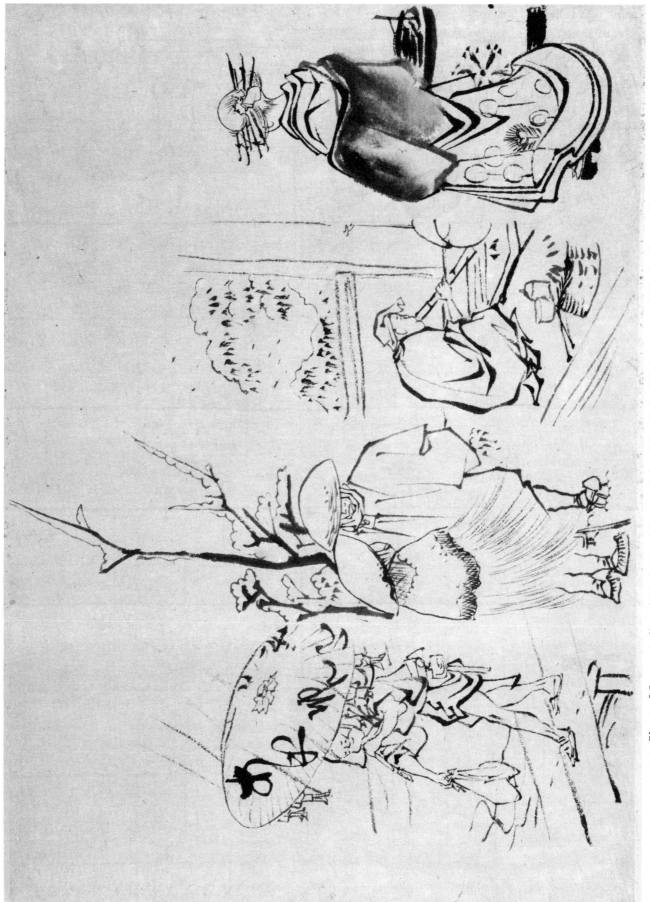

23. Sheet of figure studies. *Metropolitan Museum of Art, New York. Gift in memory of Charles Stewart Smith, 1914.*

24. Miscellaneous studies. *Manga*, Vol. 8, 1818. Woodcut. $7 \times 4\frac{7}{8}$ in. *Author's collection*.

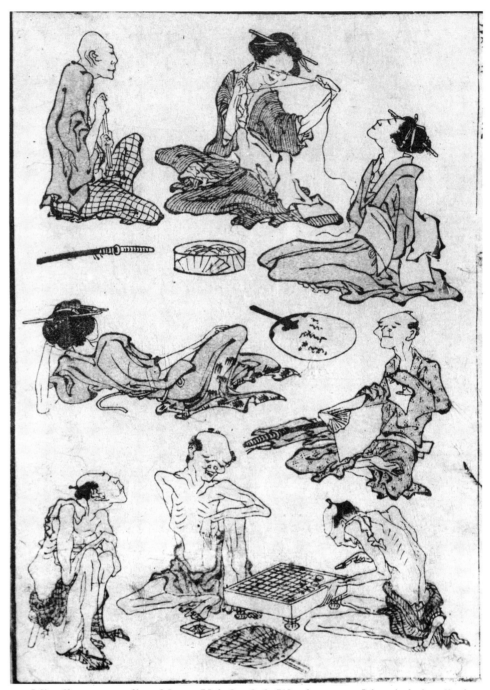

25. Miscellaneous studies. *Manga*, Vol. 8, 1818. Woodcut. $7 \times 4\frac{7}{8}$ in. *Author's collection*.

26. Pedestrians in a sudden shower. From the "Day" series. $3\frac{11}{16} \times 10\frac{3}{8}$ in. *Museum of Fine Arts, Boston.*

27. Labourers raising a pole bearing a votive banner. From the "Night" series. $3\frac{11}{16} \times 10\frac{3}{8}$ in. *Museum of Fine Arts, Boston.*

28. End of the year preparations. From the "Day" series. $3\frac{11}{16} \times 5\frac{3}{16}$ in.
Museum of Fine Arts, Boston.

29. Strolling musicians and a man with a box. From the "Night" series. $3\frac{11}{16} \times 5\frac{3}{16}$ in.
Museum of Fine Arts, Boston.

30. Palanquin in the snow. From the "Night" series. $3\frac{11}{16} \times 5\frac{3}{16}$ in.
Museum of Fine Arts, Boston.

31. Travellers in the snow. From the "Night" series. $3\frac{11}{16} \times 5\frac{3}{16}$ in.
Museum of Fine Arts, Boston.

32. Umbrella-makers. From the "Day" series. $3\frac{11}{16} \times 10\frac{3}{8}$ in. *Museum of Fine Arts, Boston.*

33. Men rolling *sake* casks. From the "Day" series. $3\frac{11}{16} \times 10\frac{3}{8}$ in. *Museum of Fine Arts, Boston.*

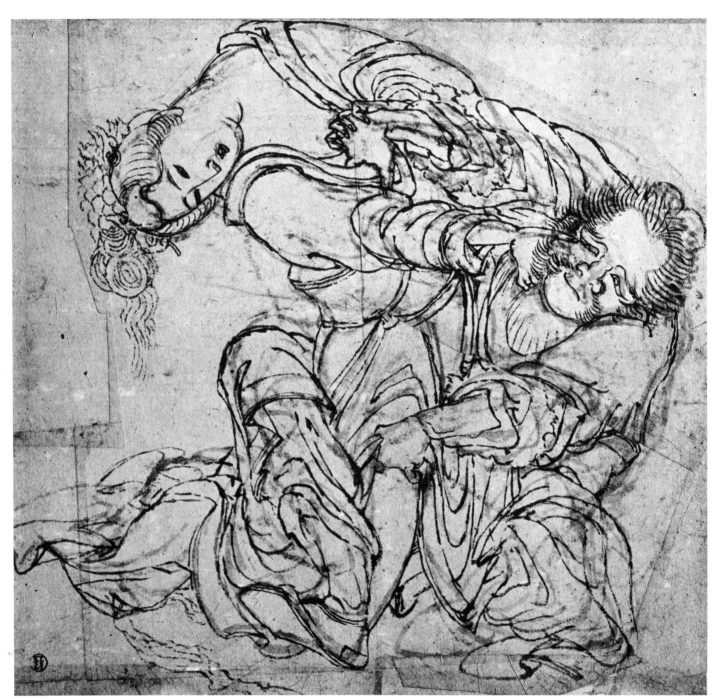

34. "The Rape". Study for plate 35. $11\frac{7}{8} \times 11\frac{7}{8}$ in. *Musée Guimet, Paris.*

35. Soko grappling with a woman. Woodcut from Vol. 29 of the *Shimpen Suiko Gaden*. About 1825. (See plate 34.) $7\frac{1}{2} \times 5\frac{3}{8}$ in. *Author's collection.*

36. A courtesan making a New Year visit. Painting on silk. 44 × 16⅜ in. *Freer Gallery of Art, Washington.*

37. Taito II (?): A courtesan under a cherry-tree. Painting on silk. 32½ × 9½ in. *Freer Gallery of Art, Washington.*

元人貌耐菴水滸
一百二十四圖

38. Half-length study of one of the "Heroes of Suikoden". Preparatory drawing for an illustration to *Chuji Suikoden Ehon*. "Collection of Pictures of the Heroes of Suikoden", 1829. $9\frac{3}{4} \times 6\frac{7}{8}$ in. *British Museum, London.*

40. Roji Shinsei and Gyokurin Roshungi. Woodcut from the *Chūji Suikoden Ehon*, 1829. (See plate 39.) 8½×6 in. *Author's collection.*

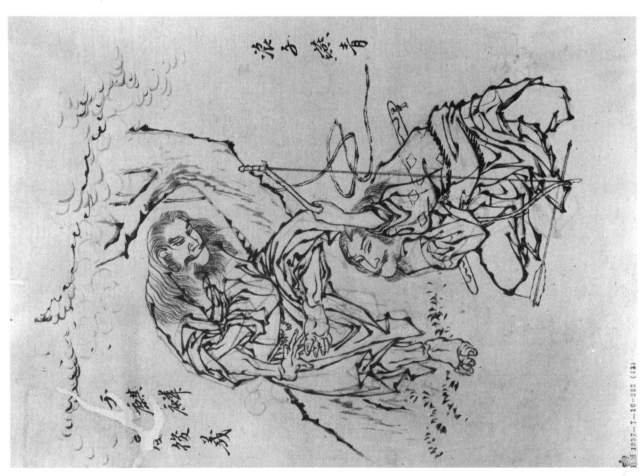

39. Roji Shinsei and Gyokurin Roshungi, two of the "Heroes". Preparatory drawing for plate 40. *British Museum, London.*

41. The Heroes of Suikoden, part of a *makimono*. $15\frac{7}{8}$ in. high. *Freer Gallery of Art, Washington.*

42. "Worship at the Hour of the Ox". Preparatory drawing for plate 43.
From a sketchbook in the *Bibliothèque Nationale, Paris.*

43. "Worship at the Hour of the Ox". Woodcut from the book *Hokusai Onna Imagawa* (see plate 42), n.d. *c.* 1830.
$7\frac{1}{2} \times 10\frac{3}{4}$ in. *Author's collection.*

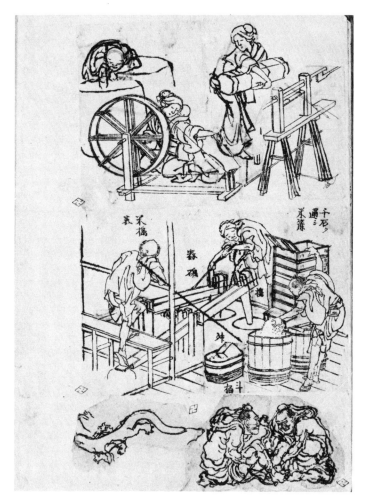

44. Spinning, rice-paste making, and other sketches.
From an album in *Bibliothèque Nationale, Paris.*

45. An incident from a Chinese romance. Preparatory drawing for a book illustration. From the same album as plate 44. *Bibliothèque Nationale, Paris.*

46. An old man singing, a girl accompanying him on a *samisen*. $9 \times 11\frac{1}{2}$ in. *Private collection, Italy.*

47. Pounding rice-paste. Perhaps a first draught for a design which appeared in *Hokusai Gashiki*, published in 1819. $16\frac{1}{2} \times 21\frac{3}{4}$ in. *Metropolitan Museum of Art, New York.*

48. Badger and kettle. 35 × 10¾ in. *Ralph Harari Collection, London.*

49. Cock and hen. 24¼ × 17⅜ in. *Mr. and Mrs. Eliot Hodgkin Collection, London.*

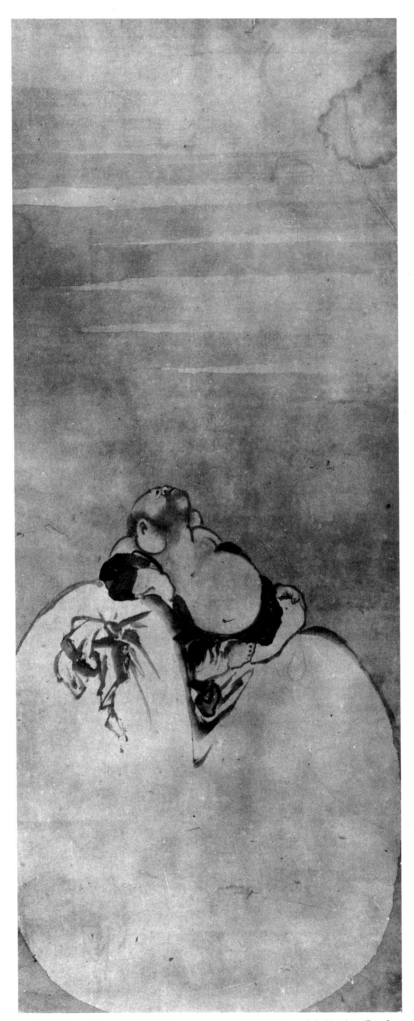

50. Hotei and his sack. Painting on paper. *Ralph Harari Collection, London.*

51. Mount Fuji and Enoshima. Two-fold screen, painting on paper. $64\frac{3}{4} \times 62\frac{1}{2}$ in. *Freer Gallery of Art, Washington.*

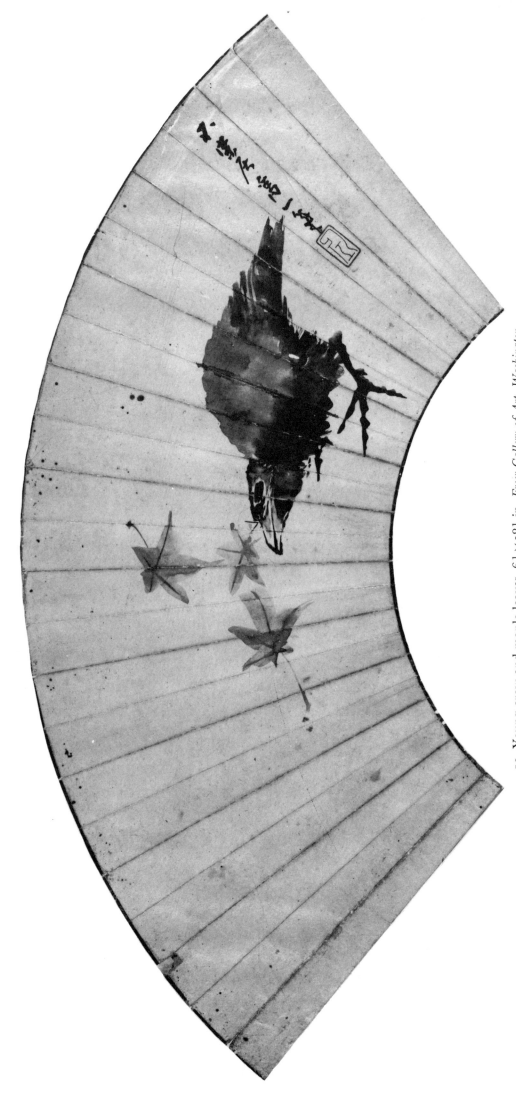

52. Young crow and maple leaves. $6\frac{1}{2} \times 18\frac{1}{8}$ in. *Freer Gallery of Art, Washington.*

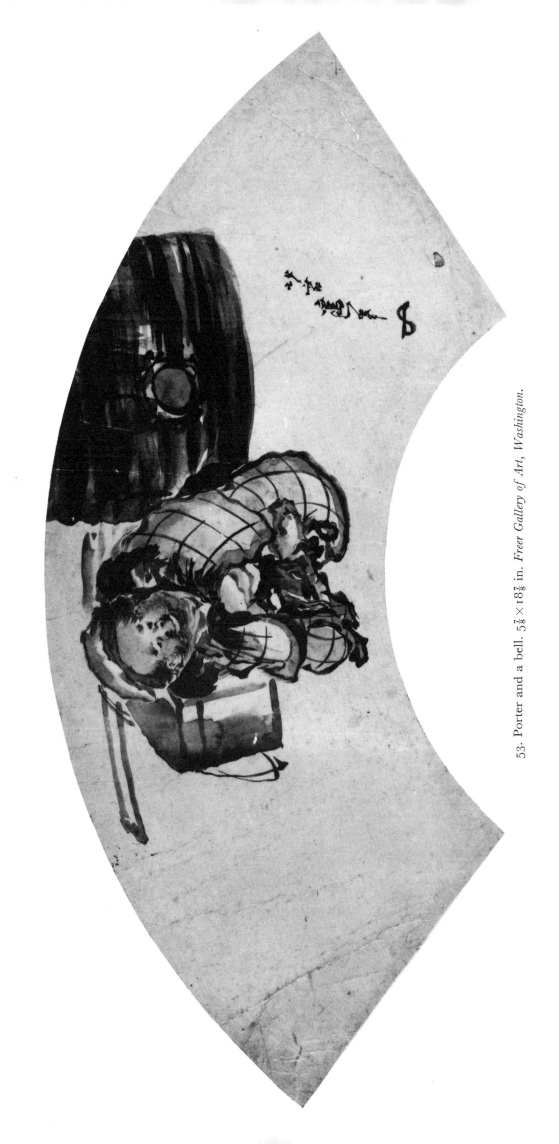

53. Porter and a bell. $5\frac{7}{8} \times 18\frac{7}{8}$ in. *Freer Gallery of Art, Washington.*

54. Flowering gourd and a bee. 14¼×22 in. *Freer Gallery of Art, Washington.*

55. Gourd leaves, flowers and moth. *Nathan Chaikin Collection.*

56. Seated girl with a long tobacco pipe. *Nathan Chaikin Collection.*

57. Mother and child. *Victoria and Albert Museum, London.*

58. Woman holding wad of handkerchiefs between her teeth. *Nathan Chaikin Collection.*

59. Sambaso dancer. *Freer Gallery of Art, Washington.*

60. Standing girl tying her head-dress. 12⅜ ×9 in. *Freer Gallery of Art, Washington.*

61. Girl playing *samisen* and another figure. *Freer Gallery of Art, Washington.*

62. Boy spinning a top. $4\frac{1}{2} \times 3\frac{7}{8}$ in. *Huguette Berès, Paris.*

63. Old couple seated. $9 \times 11\frac{1}{2}$ in. *Private Collection, Italy.*

64. Lion-dance troupe. 10⅝ × 14¹⁵⁄₁₆ in. *Freer Gallery of Art, Washington.*

65. Studies of two reclining girls. $9\frac{1}{4} \times 12\frac{3}{4}$ in. *Metropolitan Museum of Art, New York. Gift in memory of Charles Stewart Smith.*

66. Two studies of a man in his cups ("Summer relaxation"). 12⅜×9¼ in. *Freer Gallery of Art, Washington.*

67. Two zanies, a warrior and a priest. 12 $\frac{13}{16}$ ×9$\frac{5}{16}$ in. *Freer Gallery of Art, Washington.*

68. Preparatory drawing for a colour-print in the series *Hyakunin Isshu Ubaga Etoki*. "The One-hundred poems explained by the nurse" (the poet: Dainagon Kinto). 10 × 14½ in. *Freer Gallery of Art, Washington*.

69. Preparatory drawing for a colour-print in the series *Hyakunin Isshu Ubaga Etoki* (the poet: Jakuren Hoshi). $10 \times 14\frac{5}{8}$ in. *Freer Gallery of Art, Washington.*

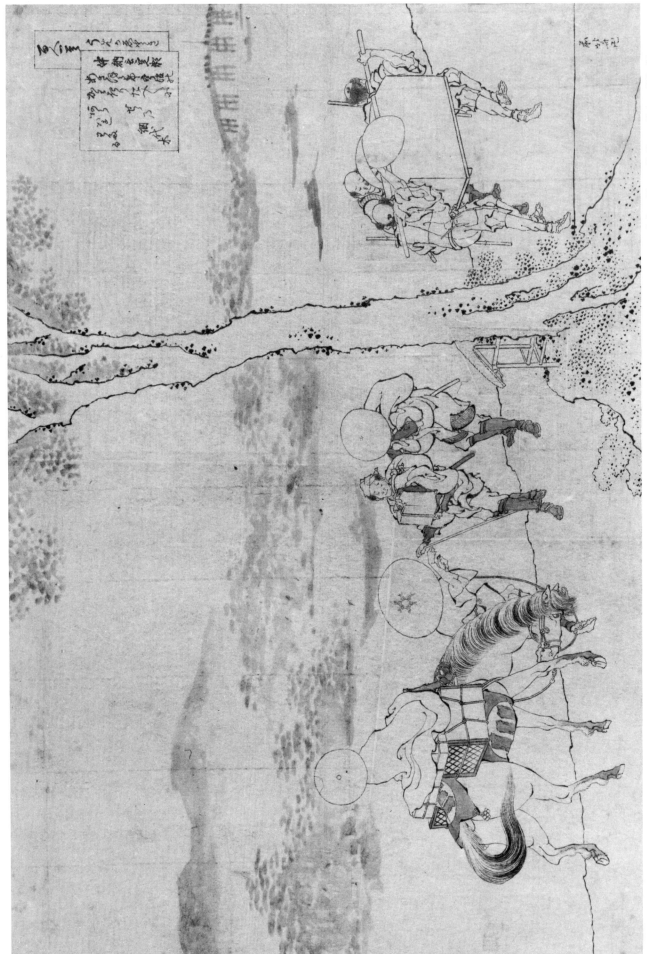

70. Preparatory drawing for a colour-print in the series *Hyakunin Isshu Ubaga Etoki* (the poet: Chunagon Sadayori). 10 × 14⅝ in. *Freer Gallery of Art, Washington.*

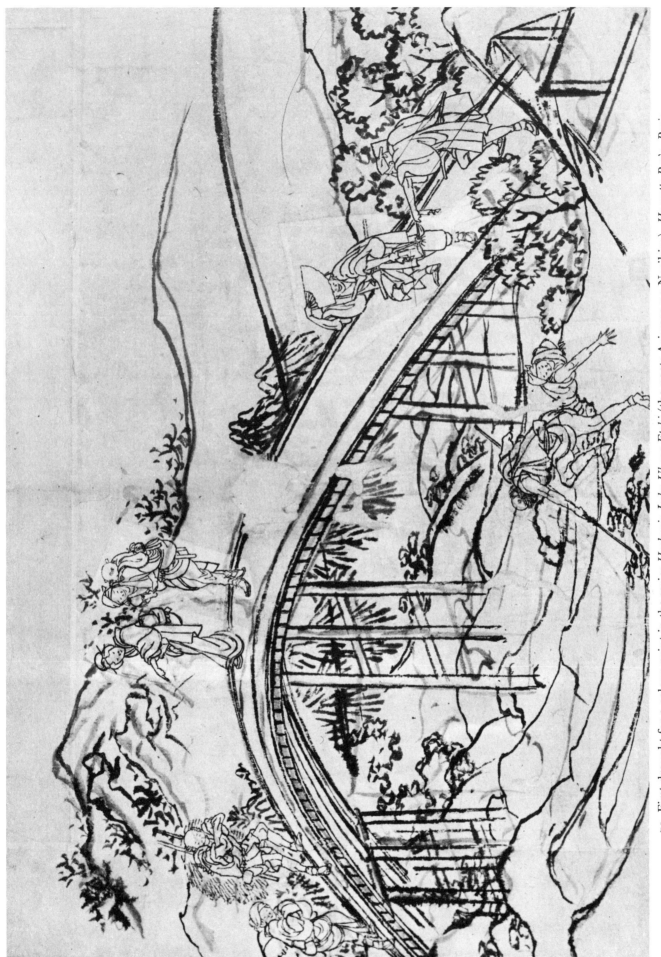

71. First draught for a colour-print in the series *Hyakunin Isshu Ubaga Etoki* (the poet: Ariwara no Narihira). *Huguette Berès, Paris.*

72. The Sparrow Dance. *Nathan Chaikin Collection.*

73. Another group of Sparrow-dancers. *Nathan Chaikin Collection.*

74. Seated woman. *Louvre, Paris.*

75. Merchant. 10 13/16 × 8 9/16 in. *Freer Gallery of Art, Washington.*

76. Assistant kneeling before the principal performer wearing a *shishi*-mask.
Drawing for the 3rd month 24th day from the *Nisshin Joma* album. 1843.
6¾ in. deep. *Sho Miyamoto Collection, Tokyo.*

77. Dog barking at a performer in a *shishi*-mask. Drawing for 4th month 8th day from the *Nisshin Joma* album. 1843.
6¾×9½ in. *Sho Miyamoto Collection, Tokyo.*

78. Two boys performing in the *shishi-mai* (the Lion Dance). Drawing for the 2nd month 3rd day from the *Nisshin Joma* album. 1843. 6¾×9½ in. *Sho Miyamoto Collection, Tokyo.*

79. *Shishi* leaping. Drawing for the 6th month 6th day from the *Nisshin Joma* album. 1843. 6¾×9½ in. *Sho Miyamoto Collection, Tokyo.*

80. Sleeping girl. *Nathan Chaikin Collection.*

82. Fish-head and plum-branch, and fox-monk with trap. Section of a *makimo*

81. Woodman. $7\frac{7}{16} \times 10\frac{9}{16}$ in. *Freer Gallery of Art, Washington.*

miscellaneous drawings. $10\frac{1}{2}$ in. high. 1839. *Freer Gallery of Art, Washington.*

四ツ谷

眼鏡ヲカヽ

橋本町

83. Festival scenes from the "Life in the Eastern Capital" album. 7 × 9½ in. *Shozaburo Watanabe Collection, Tokyo.*

84. Street and market scene. From the "Life in the Eastern Capital" album. 7×9½ in. *Shozaburo Watanabe Collection, Tokyo.*

85. Warrior with glaive. 28 × 11 in. *Ralph Harari Collection, London.*

86. Standing warrior. 28 × 11 in. *Ralph Harari Collection, London.*

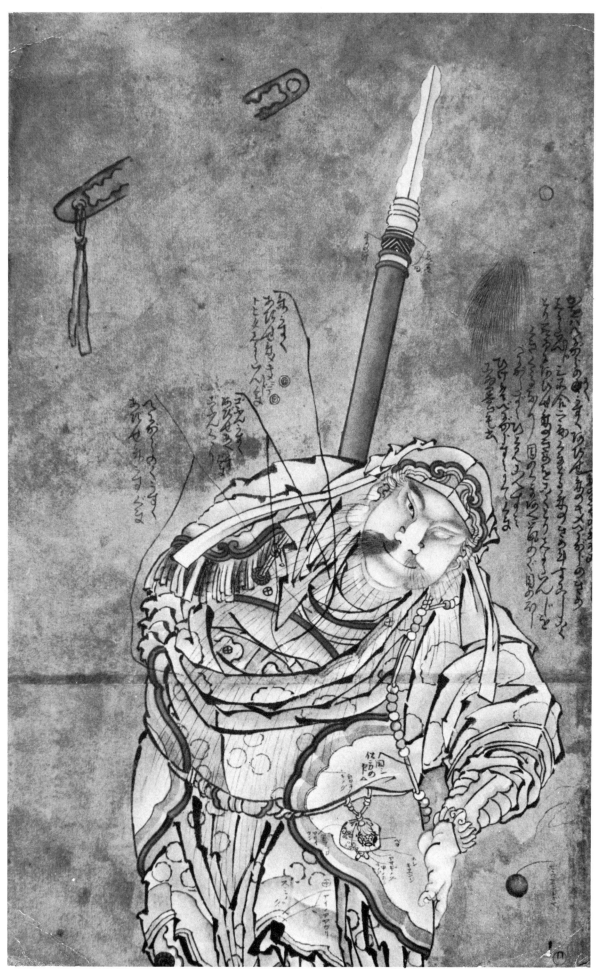

87. Warrior. Detail from drawing with inscription outlining method of painting. 11 in. wide.
Ralph Harari Collection, London.

88. Pine on a bank with grazing goats below. 28 × 11 in.
Ralph Harari Collection, London.

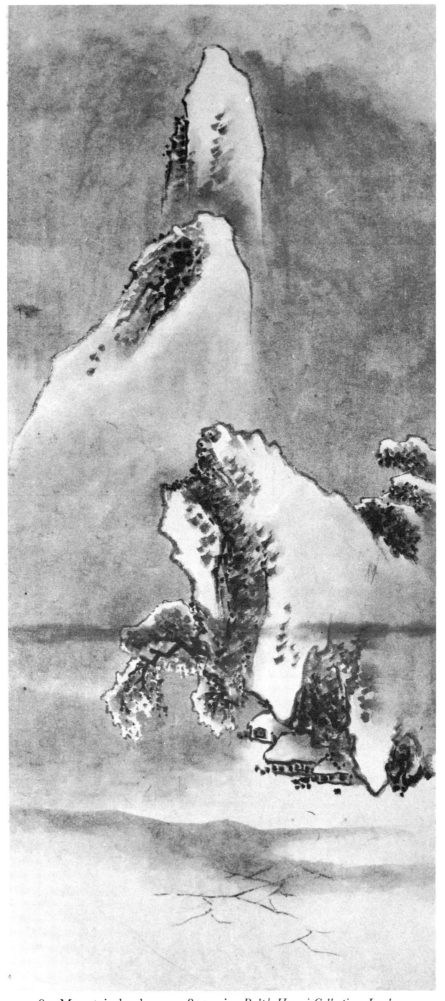

89. Mountain landscape. 28 × 11 in. *Ralph Harari Collection, London.*

90. Fisherman with net. 28 × 11 in. *Ralph Harari Collection,
London.*

91. Woodman resting on his axe. 1849. Painting on silk.
$44\frac{7}{8} \times 15\frac{7}{16}$ in. *Freer Gallery of Art, Washington.*

92. Taito II: Peasant with mattock and duck. Sealed Hokusen. 8¼ × 12½ in.
Victoria and Albert Museum, London.

93. Taito II: Girl playing a *samisen*. 6¼ × 8½ in. *Victoria and Albert Museum, London.*

94. Hokusai or Taito II: Cormorant-fishing. *Kakemono.*
50¼ × 14¼ in. *Hakone Museum, Japan.*

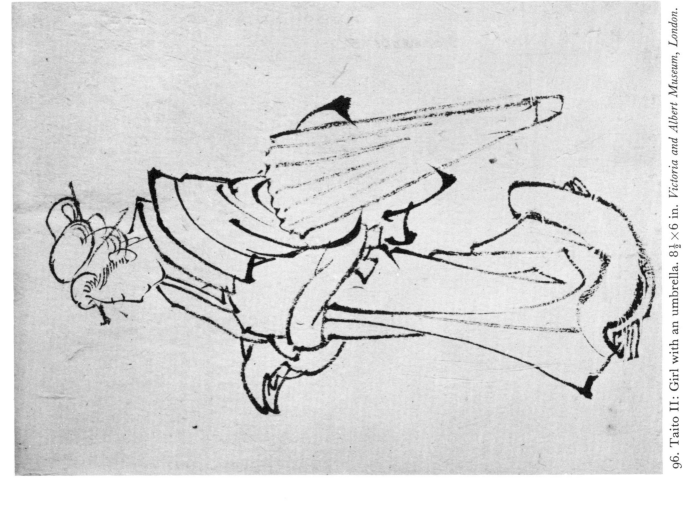

96. Taito II: Girl with an umbrella. $8\frac{1}{2} \times 6$ in. *Victoria and Albert Museum, London.*

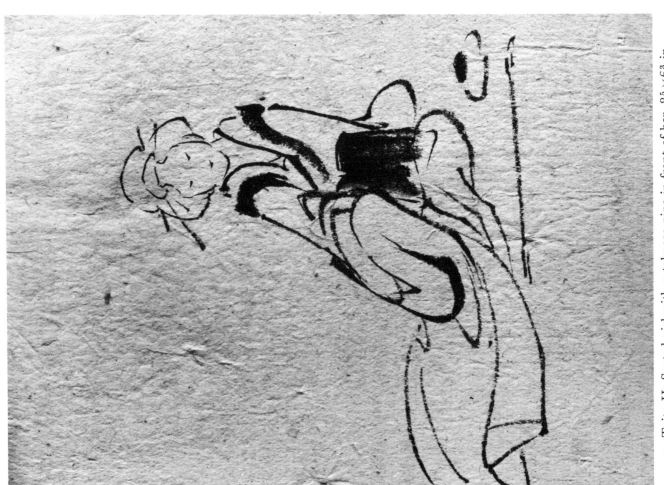

95. Taito II: Seated girl with a tobacco-pipe in front of her. $8\frac{5}{8} \times 6\frac{3}{8}$ in. *Victoria and Albert Museum, London.*

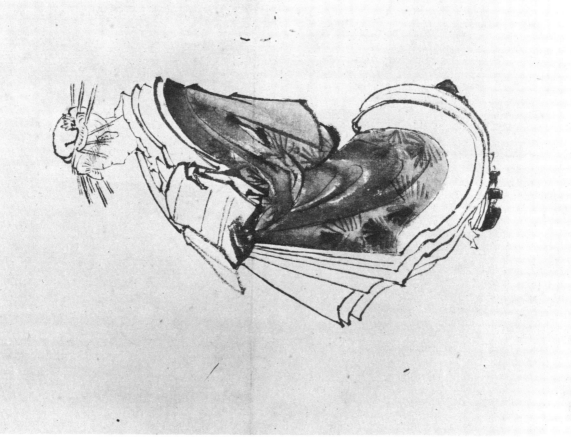

97. Taito II: Colour-print of a courtesan from
Harimaze han, 1843 (see plate 98). *Author's collection.*

98. Taito II: Study for plate 97. *Victoria and Albert Museum, London.*

99. Taito II: Men hauling on a rope and other studies. 9½ × 13 in. *Victoria and Albert Museum, London.*

100. School of Hokusai: page of miscellaneous drawings from an album. 10 × 14 in. *Honolulu Academy of Arts, Honolulu, Hawaii.*

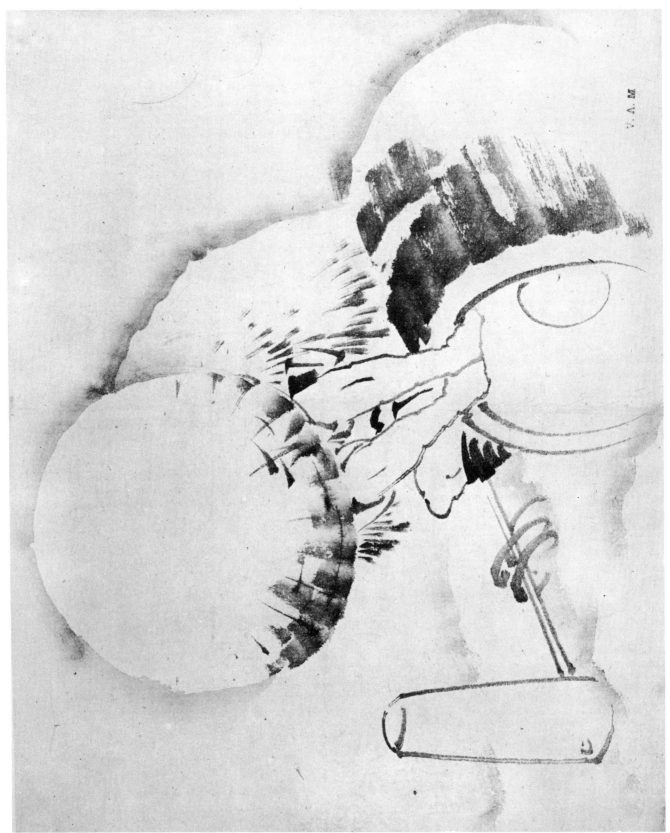

101. Taigaku: Man pulling a mortar out of the snow. $7\frac{1}{2} \times 9\frac{3}{4}$ in. *Victoria and Albert Museum, London.*

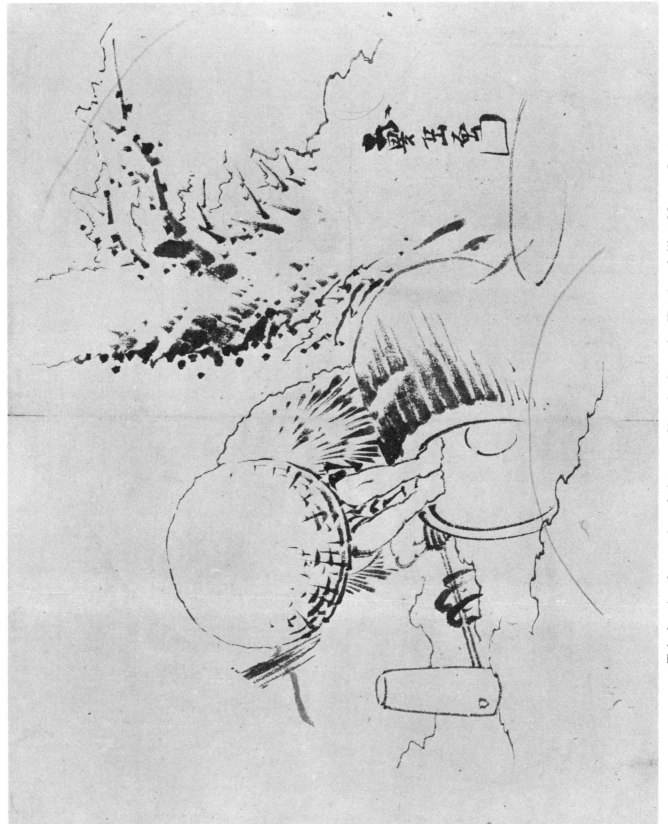

102. Taigaku: Another version of plate 101. Signed. $7\frac{5}{8} \times 11$ in. *Victoria and Albert Museum, London.*

103. Hokkei: Study of a store, with a man counting on an abacus. $7\frac{3}{8} \times 5$ in.
Victoria and Albert Museum, London.

104. Hokkei: Reclining girl reading a letter. 9 × 18½ in. *Victoria and Albert Museum, London.*

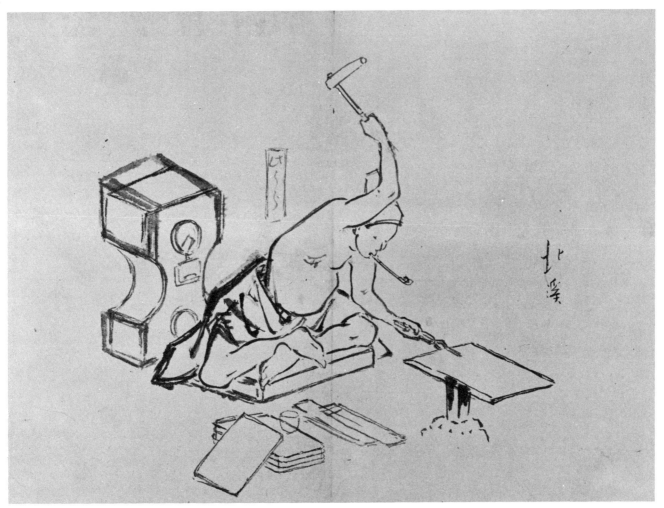

105. Hokkei: Metal-worker at his forge. 7⅝ × 11 in. *Victoria and Albert Museum, London.*

106. Hokkei: Crow and shells. $12\frac{1}{4} \times 10\frac{7}{8}$ in. *Art Institute of Chicago.*

107. Hokuba: Peasant girl with torn umbrella. $37\frac{1}{2} \times 10\frac{3}{4}$ in. *Ralph Harari Collection, London.*

108. Hokuba: Girl greeting a man at the open door of a house. 14 × 10⅝ in. *Art Institute of Chicago*.

109. Hokuba: Domestic scene with a woman at the wash-tub. $14 \times 10\frac{5}{8}$ in. *Art Institute of Chicago*.

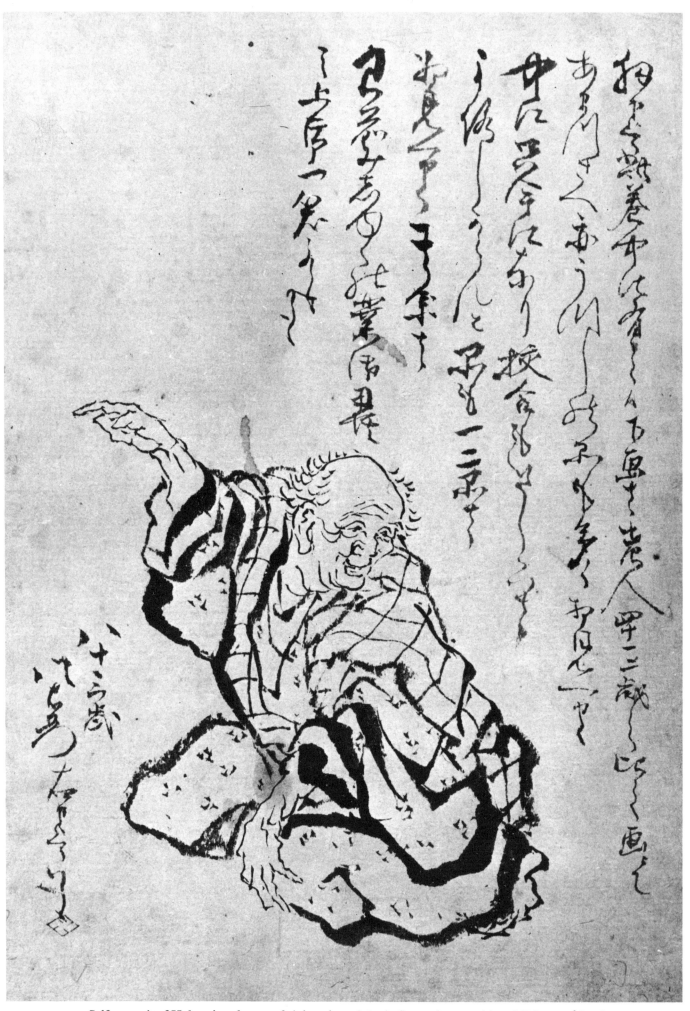

110. Self-portrait of Hokusai at the age of eighty-three (1842), from a letter to his publisher. 10½ in. deep.
Rijksmuseum voor Volkenkunde, Leiden, Holland.

Bibliography

Acknowledgements

List of Plates

Bibliography

GONSE, L., *L'Art Japonais*. Paris, 1883.

ANDERSON, W., *Descriptive and historical catalogue of a collection of Japanese and Chinese Paintings in the British Museum*. London, 1886.

ANDERSON, W., *The Pictorial Arts of Japan*. London, 1886.

HUISH, M. B., *Catalogue of a collection of Drawings and Engravings by Hokusai Exhibited at the Fine Art Society*. Introductory note by Marcus B. Huish. London, 1890.

FENOLLOSA, E. F., *Boston Museum of Fine Arts, Department of Japanese Art. Special Exhibition of the Pictorial Art of Japan and China. No. 1: Hokusai and his School*. Boston, 1893.

JIJIMA, HANJURO, *Katsushika Hokusai den*. Tokyo, 1893.

GONCOURT, E. DE. 'Hokousai. Ses albums traitant de la peinture et du dessin, avec ses préfaces'. *Gazette des Beaux-Arts*. Paris, 1895.

GONCOURT, E. DE, *Hokousai*. Paris, 1896.

FENOLLOSA, E. F., *Catalogue of the Exhibition of Paintings of Hokusai Held at Japan Fine Art Association, Uyeno Park, Tokio, from 13th to 30th January, 1900*. Tokyo, 1901.

PERZYNSKI, F., *Hokusai*. Bielefeld and Leipzig, 1904.

STRANGE, E. F., *Hokusai*. London, 1906.

ROTHENSTEIN, W., *Two Drawings by Hok'sai. From the Collection of W. Rothenstein*. Broad Campden, Glos., 1910.

MORRISON, A., *The Painters of Japan*. London, 1911.

FOCILLON, H., *Hokousai*. Paris, 1914.

INOUE, K., *The relationship between Hokusai and his pupil Hokusen who took over the name Taito when Hokusai relinquished it*. Ukiyoeshi, Tokyo, 1929.

MIZUTANI, Y., *Kohan Shosetsu Soga Shi*. Tokyo, 1936.

MODDERMAN, E. J., *Japansche Teekeningen en Schetsen*. Exhibition in the Frans Hals Museum in Haarlem. Haarlem, 1938.

NARAZAKI, MUNESHIGE, *Hokusai Ron*. Tokyo, 1944.

GRAY, B., *British Museum. The Work of Hokusai*. Woodcuts, Illustrated Books, Drawings and Paintings: a Catalogue of an Exhibition held on the occasion of the Centenary of his Death. Introduction by Basil Gray. London, 1948.

BRUIJN, R. DE, *Hokusai, 1760–1849*. Catalogue of an exhibition of the works of Katsushika Hokusai in Holland and Belgium. Stedelyk Museum, Amsterdam, June/August, 1949. Introduction by R. de Bruijn.

GRUYTER, W. J. DE, *Rembrandt, Hokusai and van Gogh*. Catalogue of an exhibition of drawings at the Stedelyk Museum, Amsterdam, October/November, 1951. Introduction by W. Jos. de Gruyter. Amsterdam, 1951.

GRUYTER, W. J. DE, *Hokusai. Drawings and Water-Colours*. Catalogue of the Arts Council of Great Britain Exhibition, 1954. Introduction by W. Jos. de Gruyter.

HILLIER, J., *Hokusai: Paintings, Drawings and Woodcuts*. London, 1955.

HILLIER, J., 'Hokusai: some drawings and problems of attribution'. *The Connoisseur*. London, May, 1956.

HILLIER, J., 'Drawings by Hokusai's followers: Taito and Hokkei'. *The Connoisseur*. London, May/June, 1957.

TOMITA, K., *Day and Night in the Four Seasons by Hokusai*. Museum of Fine Arts, Boston, 1957.

HILLIER, J., *Hokusai, dessins, aquarelles, estampes, livres*. An exhibition at the gallery of Huguette Berès, Paris, June/July, 1958. Introduction by J. Hillier.

HILLIER, J., 'Hokusai drawings in the Harari Collection'. *The Connoisseur*. London, June, 1960.

(STERN, HAROLD P.) *Hokusai: Paintings and Drawings in the Freer Gallery of Art, Smithsonian Institution*. Washington, 1960.

BOWIE, THEODORE, 'Hokusai and the comic tradition in Japanese painting'. *College Art Journal*, XIX, 3 (Spring, 1960).

FONTEIN, J. *Het Landschap bij Hokusai*. Exhibition at the Rijksprentenkabinet, Amsterdam, September/December, 1962. Introduction by J. Fontein.

BOWIE, THEODORE, *The Drawings of Hokusai*. Indiana University Press. Bloomington, 1964.

KANEKO, FUSHI, *Hokusai-O Shinrabansho Gashu*. Tokyo, 1964.

Acknowledgements

The author is grateful to a number of friends for permission to reproduce drawings and paintings in their possession, namely Madame Berès, Mr. Nathan Chaikin, Mr. Ralph Harari, and Mr. and Mrs. Eliot Hodgkin. He has a particular debt to Mr. C. H. Mitchell of Tokyo and Mr. Shigetaka Kaneko of the Tokyo National Museum for enlisting the interest of Mr. Sho Miyamoto and Mr. Shozaburo Watanabe, whose generous response is acknowledged with thanks. Thanks are also due to the authorities and Trustees at the Bibliothèque Nationale, Paris; the Museum of Fine Arts, Boston; the British Museum, London; the Art Institute of Chicago; the Smithsonian Institution, the Freer Gallery of Art, Washington; the Hakone Museum, Japan; the Musée du Louvre, Paris; the Metropolitan Museum of Art, New York; the Honolulu Academy of Arts; the Rijksmuseum voor Volkenkunde, Leiden, Holland; and the Victoria and Albert Museum, London.

Tribute is also paid to the benefit received from stimulating correspondence and discussion with Dr. Harold P. Stern of the Freer Gallery, and Prof. Theodore Bowie of Indiana University; the author respects their profound knowledge of Hokusai even if he has not always been in agreement with their views.

Author and publisher express their thanks to the Editor of *The Connoisseur* for permission to re-use material which appeared in a series of articles in that magazine in 1956, 1957 and 1960.

LIST OF PLATES

BOSTON, *Museum of Fine Arts*

26. Pedestrians in a sudden shower. From the 'Day' series. $3\frac{11}{16} \times 10\frac{3}{8}$ in.
27. Labourers raising a pole bearing a votive banner. From the 'Night' series. $3\frac{11}{16} \times 10\frac{3}{8}$ in.
28. End of the year preparations. From the 'Day' series. $3\frac{11}{16} \times 5\frac{3}{16}$ in.
29–31. Strolling musicians and a man with a box. Palanquin in the snow. Travellers in the snow. From the 'Night' series. $3\frac{11}{16} \times 5\frac{3}{16}$ in.
32–33. Umbrella-makers. Men rolling *sake* casks. From the 'Day' series. $3\frac{11}{16} \times 10\frac{3}{8}$ in.

CHICAGO, *Art Institute*

106. Hokkei: Crow and shells. $12\frac{1}{4} \times 10\frac{7}{8}$ in.
108. Hokuba: Girl greeting a man at the open door of a house. $14 \times 10\frac{5}{8}$ in.
109. Hokuba: Domestic scene with a woman at the wash-tub. $14 \times 10\frac{5}{8}$ in.

HAKONE, *Japan, Museum*

1. Girl making up at a mirror. Painting on paper. 53×20 in.
94. Hokusai or Taito II: Cormorant fishing. *Kakemono.* $50\frac{1}{4} \times 14\frac{1}{4}$ in.

HONOLULU, *Academy of Arts*

100. School of Hokusai: page of miscellaneous drawings from an album. 10×14 in.

LEIDEN, *Rijksmuseum voor Volkenkunde*

110. Self-portrait of Hokusai at the age of eighty-three (1842), from a letter to his publisher.

LONDON, *British Museum*

22. The Mad Poet. From a sheet of studies. $10\frac{1}{2} \times 15\frac{3}{4}$ in.
38. Half-length study of one of the 'Heroes of Suikoden'. Preparatory drawing for an illustration to *Chuji Suikoden Ehon*. 'Collection of Pictures of the Heroes of Suikoden', 1829. $9\frac{3}{4} \times 6\frac{7}{8}$ in.
39. Roji Shinsei and Gyokurin Roshungi, two of the 'Heroes'. Preparatory drawing.

LONDON, *Victoria and Albert Museum*

12. Wagtail and reed. $11\frac{1}{4} \times 15$ in.
57. Mother and child.
92. Taito II: Peasant with mattock and duck. Sealed Hokusen. $8\frac{1}{4} \times 12\frac{1}{2}$ in.
93. Taito II: Girl playing a *samisen*. $6\frac{1}{4} \times 8\frac{1}{2}$ in.
95. Taito II: Seated girl with a tobacco-pipe in front of her. $8\frac{5}{8} \times 6\frac{3}{8}$ in.
96. Taito II: Girl with an umbrella. $8\frac{1}{2} \times 6$ in.
98. Taito II: A Courtesan.

99. Taito II: Men hauling on a rope and other studies. $9\frac{1}{2} \times 13$ in.
101. Taigaku: Man pulling a mortar out of the snow. $7\frac{1}{2} \times 9\frac{3}{4}$ in.
102. Taigaku: Another version of pl. 101. Signed. $7\frac{5}{8} \times 11$ in.
103. Hokkei: Study of a store, with a man counting on an abacus. $7\frac{3}{8} \times 5$ in.
104. Hokkei: Reclining girl reading a letter. $9 \times 18\frac{1}{2}$ in.
105. Hokkei: Metal-worker at his forge. $7\frac{5}{8} \times 11$ in.

LONDON, *Ralph Harari Collection*

5. Courtesan strolling under a full moon, verse by Santo Kyoden. $57\frac{7}{8} \times 16$ in.
6. Branch of flowering plum. 46×14 in.
17. Porters at a quayside. From the 'Occupations' album, 1811. 11×15 in.
18. Ferry-boat in the Snow. From the 'Occupations' album, 1811. 11×15 in.
19. Festival lantern makers. From the 'Occupations' album, 1811. 11×15 in.
20. Group of villagers beside a cottage, others crossing a footbridge. From the 'Occupations' album, 1811. 11×15 in.
48. Badger and kettle. $35 \times 10\frac{3}{4}$ in.
50. Hotei and his sack. Painting on paper.
85. Warrior with glaive. 28×11 in.
86. Standing warrior. 28×11 in.
87. Warrior. Detail from drawing with inscription outlining method of painting. 11 in. wide.
88. Pine on a bank with grazing goats below. 28×11 in.
89. Mountain landscape. 28×11 in.
90. Fisherman with net. 28×11 in.
107. Hokuba: Peasant girl with torn umbrella. $37\frac{1}{2} \times 10\frac{3}{4}$ in.

LONDON, *Mr. and Mrs. Eliot Hodgkin Collection*

49. Cock and hen. $24\frac{1}{4} \times 17\frac{3}{8}$ in.

NEW YORK, *Metropolitan Museum of Art*

7. Woman dressing her hair. $10\frac{1}{8} \times 6\frac{1}{2}$ in.
14. Acrobat performing with swords before a crowd.
15. Posting-station beside a river. $9\frac{1}{4} \times 13$ in. Preparatory drawing for one of the illustrations to Rokujuen's novel *Hida-no-takumi*, 'The Craftsman of Hida', 1808.
16. Tile-makers working by their kilns. $15 \times 11\frac{1}{2}$ in.
23. Sheet of figure studies.
47. Pounding rice-paste. Perhaps a first draft for a design which appeared in *Hokusai Gashiki*, published in 1819. $16\frac{1}{2} \times 21\frac{3}{4}$ in.
65. Studies of two reclining girls. $9\frac{1}{4} \times 12\frac{3}{4}$ in.

PARIS, *Musée du Louvre*

74. Seated Woman.

PARIS, *Bibliothèque Nationale*

42. 'Worship at the Hour of the Ox.' Preparatory drawing. From an album.

44. Spinning, rice-paste making, and other sketches. From the same album as pl. 42.
45. An incident from a Chinese romance. Preparatory drawing for a book illustration. From the same album as pl. 42.

PARIS, *Musée Guimet*

34. 'The Rape.' Study. $11\frac{7}{8} \times 11\frac{7}{8}$ in.

PARIS, *Huguette Berès*

21. The Mad Poet. From a sheet of studies. $7\frac{1}{8} \times 15\frac{7}{8}$ in.
62. Boy spinning a top. $4\frac{1}{2} \times 3\frac{7}{8}$ in.
71. First draught for a colour-print in the series *Hyakunin Isshu Ubaga Etoki* (the poet: Ariwara no Narihira).

TOKYO, *Sho Miyamoto Collection*

76. Assistant kneeling before the principal performer wearing a *shishi*-mask. Drawing for the 3rd month 24th day from the *Nisshin Joma* album. 1843. $6\frac{3}{4} \times 9\frac{1}{2}$ in.
77. Dog barking at a performer in a *shishi*-mask. Drawing for 4th month 8th day from the *Nisshin Joma* album. 1843. $6\frac{3}{4} \times 9\frac{1}{2}$ in.
78. Two boys performing in the *shishi-mai* (the Lion Dance). Drawing for the 2nd month 3rd day from the *Nisshin Joma* album, 1843. $6\frac{3}{4} \times 9\frac{1}{2}$ in.
79. *Shishi* leaping. Drawing for the 6th month 6th day from the *Nisshin Joma* album, 1843. $6\frac{3}{4} \times 9\frac{1}{2}$ in.

TOKYO, *Shozaburo Watanabe Collection*

83. Festival scenes from the 'Life in the Eastern Capital' album. $7 \times 9\frac{1}{2}$ in.
84. Street and market scene. From the 'Life in the Eastern Capital' album. $7 \times 9\frac{1}{2}$ in.

WASHINGTON, D.C., *Freer Gallery of Art*

2. An effeminate fop. $20 \times 8\frac{1}{2}$ in.
3. Daikoku and Ebisu as New Year Performers. 7×18 in.
4. The Six Master Poets. $12\frac{3}{4} \times 22\frac{3}{16}$ in.
8. Flowering plum branches. $7\frac{1}{8} \times 18\frac{1}{8}$ in.
9. Landscape. $11 \times 23\frac{1}{2}$ in.
36. A courtesan making a New Year visit. Painting on silk. $44 \times 16\frac{3}{8}$ in.
37. Taito II (?): A courtesan under a cherry tree. Painting on silk. $32\frac{1}{2} \times 9\frac{1}{2}$ in.
41. The Heroes of Suikoden, part of a *makimono*. $15\frac{7}{8}$ in. high.
51. Mount Fuji and Enoshima. Two-fold screen, painting on paper. $64\frac{3}{4} \times 62\frac{1}{2}$ in.
52. Young crow and maple leaves. $6\frac{1}{2} \times 18\frac{1}{8}$ in.
53. Porter and a bell. $5\frac{7}{8} \times 18\frac{7}{8}$ in.
54. Flowering gourd and a bee. $14\frac{1}{4} \times 22$ in.
59. Sambaso dancer.
60. Standing girl tying her head-dress. $12\frac{3}{8} \times 9$ in.
61. Girl playing *samisen* and another figure.
64. Lion-dance troupe. $10\frac{5}{8} \times 14\frac{15}{16}$ in.
66. Two studies of a man in his cups ('Summer relaxation'). $12\frac{3}{8} \times 9\frac{1}{4}$ in.
67. Two zanies, a warrior and a priest. $12\frac{13}{16} \times 9\frac{5}{16}$ in.

68–70. Preparatory drawings for colour-prints in the series *Hyakunin Isshu Ubaga Etoki*, 'The One-hundred Poems explained by the Nurse' (the poets: Dainagon Kinto, Jakuren Hoshi), Chunagon Sadayori). $10 \times 14\frac{5}{8}$ in.

75. Merchant. $10\frac{13}{16} \times 8\frac{9}{16}$ in.
81. Woodman. $7\frac{7}{16} \times 10\frac{9}{16}$ in.
82. Fish-head and plum-branch, and fox-monk with trap. Section of a *makimono* of miscellaneous drawings. $10\frac{1}{2}$ in. high. 1839.
91. Woodman resting on his axe. 1849. Painting on silk. $44\frac{7}{8} \times 15\frac{7}{16}$ in.

Nathan Chaikin Collection

10. Woodman. $8 \times 10\frac{1}{2}$ in.
11. Crow flying against the sun. $9\frac{3}{8} \times 11\frac{3}{4}$ in.
55. Gourd leaves, flowers and moth.
56. Seated girl with a long tobacco pipe.
58. Woman holding a wad of handkerchiefs between her teeth.

72–73. Sparrow-dancers.

80. Sleeping girl.

Private Collection, Italy

13. Pheasant in the snow. Possibly a study for the print in the *Shashin Gafu*, an album datable to 1814. 11×18 in.
46. An old man singing, a girl accompanying him on a *samisen*. $9 \times 11\frac{1}{2}$ in.
63. Old couple seated. $9 \times 11\frac{1}{2}$ in.

Author's Collection

24. Miscellaneous studies. *Manga*, Vol. VIII, 1818. Woodcut. $7 \times 4\frac{7}{8}$ in.
25. Miscellaneous studies. *Manga*, Vol. VIII, 1818. Woodcut. $7 \times 4\frac{7}{8}$ in.
35. Soko grappling with a woman. Woodcut from Vol. 29 of the *Shimpen Suiko Gaden*. About 1825. $7\frac{1}{2} \times 5\frac{3}{8}$ in.
40. Roji Shinsei and Gyokurin Roshungi. Woodcut from the *Chuji Suikoden Ehon*, 1829. $8\frac{1}{2} \times 6$ in.
43. 'Worship at the Hour of the Ox.' Woodcut from the book *Hokusai Onna Imagawa* n.d. *c*. 1830. $7\frac{1}{2} \times 10\frac{3}{4}$ in.
97. Taito II: Colour-print of a courtesan from *Harimaze han*, 1843.